# TEACHER'S PET PUBLICATIONS

## PUZZLE PACK for
Touching Spirit Bear

based on the book by
Ben Mikaelsen

Written by
Beverly Schilla
Mary B. Collins

© 2010 Teacher's Pet Publications
All Rights Reserved

The materials in this packet are copyrighted
by Teacher's Pet Publications, Inc.

These pages may be duplicated by the purchaser
for use in the purchaser's own classroom.

Copying any of these materials and distributing them
for any other purpose is a violation of the copyright laws.

© 2010 Teacher's Pet Publications, Inc.
www.tpet.com

## INTRODUCTION
If you already own the LitPlan for this title, this Puzzle Pack will refresh your Unit Resource Materials and Vocabulary Resource Materials sections plus give you additional materials you can substitute into the tests. If you do not already have a complete LitPlan, these pages will give you some supplemental materials to use with your own plan. There are two main groups of materials: one set for unit words (such as characters' names, symbols, places, etc.) and one set for vocabulary words associated with the book.

## WORD LIST
There is a word list for both the unit words and the vocabulary words. These lists show you which words are being used in the materials and the clues or definitions being used for those words. You may want to give students a word list with clues/definitions to help them, or you may want students to only have a word list (without clues/definitions) if you want them to work a little harder. Both are available for duplication. The word lists can also be your "calling key" for the bingo games.

## FILL IN THE BLANK AND MATCHING
There are 4 each of the fill in the blank and matching worksheets for both the unit and vocabulary words. These pages can be used either as extra worksheets for students or as objective parts of a unit test. They can be done individually if students need extra help or as a whole class activity to review the material covered.

## MAGIC SQUARES
The magic squares not only reinforce the material covered but also work on reasoning and math skills. Many teachers have told us that their students really enjoy doing these!

## WORD SEARCH PUZZLES
The word search words go in all directions, as indicated on your answer keys. Two of the word search puzzles have the clues listed rather than the words. This makes the puzzle a little more difficult, but it reinforces the material better. Two word search puzzles have words only for students who find the clue puzzles too difficult.

## CROSSWORD PUZZLES
Both unit and vocabulary word sections have 4 crossword puzzles.

## BINGO CARDS
There are 32 individual bingo cards for the unit words and 32 individual bingo cards for the vocabulary words. You can use your word list as a "call list," calling the words at random and marking them off of your list as you go, or you could use the flash cards by cutting them apart and drawing the words at random from a hat (or box or whatever). To make a better review, you might ask for the definition and spelling of each word as you call it out–or you could call out the definitions and have students tell you the words they need to look for on the puzzle.

## JUGGLE LETTERS
The vocabulary juggle letter game is intended to help students learn the spellings of the words. One sheet has the definitions listed on it as an extra help for students who need it or to reinforce the definitions if you choose to do so.

## FLASH CARDS
We've included a set of vocabulary flash cards you can duplicate, cut, and fold for your students. Some teachers make a few sets for general use by the class; others make a set for each student. Some teachers duplicate them for each student and have the students cut & fold their own. You can cut out just the words and put them in a hat, have each student pick out one word and write the definition and a sentence for that word. Students then swap words and papers, with the next student adding a sentence of his own under the last one. You can have students swap as many times as you like. Each time the student will read the sentences written prior to his own and then add a sentence. You can cut out the words and definitions separately and play "I Have; Who Has?" Each student in the room draws a word and definition. The first student says, "I have (the name of the word). Who has the definition?" The student with the definition reads it then says, "I have (the name of the vocabulary word she has). Who has the definition?" The round continues until all words and definitions have been given.

Touching Spirit Bear Word List

1. ALASKA — the location of the island
2. ALONE — This state of being scares Cole more than anything else.
3. ANCESTOR — This rock is carried up the hill and rolled down.
4. ANGER — It is a memory never forgotten.
5. AT.ÓOW — a colorful, comforting blanket
6. BARBIE — Cole describes his mom as a scared _____.
7. BEAR — Peter ruins and then fixes Cole's carving of this.
8. BEAVER — the animal associated with lessons of persistence, patience, and ingenuity
9. BIRTHDAY — Mr. Matthews does not know Cole's _____.
10. BLACKWOOD — the lawyer hired by Cole's father
11. BLOOD — It all looks the same to Cole.
12. CAKE — Cole's wild laughter mocks the ingredients of his life's _____.
13. CHAMP — Garvey's nickname for Cole
14. CIRCLE — the last item carved on Cole's totem
15. CLUB — tiny, infecting thistles: Devil's _____
16. COLE — blames others for his life choices
17. DANCE — frequently performed as an expression of discovery
18. DYING — Cole is not afraid of this.
19. EAGLE — the animal associated with staying proud and viewing life differently from a distance
20. EDWIN — the Tlingit Elder
21. FAULT — While recovering, Cole whispers, "My _____!"
22. FEATHER — symbolizes respect
23. FISH — Cole takes and eats bits of this from the gulls.
24. FLESH — The gulls pick at Cole's
25. FORGIVES — "Until Peter _____ you, he won't heal."

| # | Term | Clue |
|---|------|------|
| 26. | GARVEY | Cole's parole officer |
| 27. | HAIR | Cole saves a handful of this but later discards it. |
| 28. | HOTDOG | All of life is like this. |
| 29. | INVISIBLE | Cole wants to learn how to be this. |
| 30. | JUSTICE | Circle _____ promotes healing. |
| 31. | KEEPER | the person in charge of Circle Justice meetings |
| 32. | KNIFE | an instrument of destruction or healing |
| 33. | MICE | They are often not noticed and see things others don't. |
| 34. | MIKAELSEN | the author of Touching Spirit Bear |
| 35. | MINNEAPOLIS | the hometown of the Matthews family |
| 36. | MOUSE | provides food and a life lesson for Cole |
| 37. | PETER | the victim of Cole's anger |
| 38. | PRIDE | There is no place for this on the island. |
| 39. | REFERRED | To Cole, this is the adult term for passing the buck. |
| 40. | ROCK | becomes both ancestor and anger |
| 41. | ROSEY | nursed Cole right after his rescue |
| 42. | SHELTER | Cole destroys it with fire. |
| 43. | SOAK | the morning ritual to clear Cole's mind |
| 44. | SPARROWS | Their instincts were for life. |
| 45. | SPIRIT | The _____ Bear mauls Cole. |
| 46. | SPIT | Cole does this at Edwin and the Spirit Bear. |
| 47. | SUICIDE | Peter attempts this twice. |
| 48. | SUPPER | "It's not about _____...You're still...looking for the easiest way to get by." |
| 49. | SWIM | Cole's first method of attempted escape |
| 50. | TENT | Cole sleeps there during Peter's visit at first. |
| 51. | TLINGIT | Edwin's native tribe |
| 52. | TOTEM | tells one's life story |

| | | |
|---|---|---|
| 53. | TRUST | Cole connects with the Spirit Bear and feels this for the first time. |
| 54. | WHALE | the animal that is graceful, powerful, and gentle |
| 55. | WILLIAM | an alcoholic child abuser |
| 56. | WOLF | the animal associated with the lesson "you need the help of others" |
| 57. | WOOD | "If you discover what's inside the _____, you'll discover what's inside of you." |
| 58. | YOURSELF | "Whatever you do to the animals, you do to _____." |

Touching Spirit Bear Fill in the Blank 1

_____  1. This state of being scares Cole more than anything else.

_____  2. Garvey's nickname for Cole

_____  3. the last item carved on Cole's totem

_____  4. They are often not noticed and see things others don't.

_____  5. Peter attempts this twice.

_____  6. becomes both ancestor and anger

_____  7. symbolizes respect

_____  8. the author of Touching Spirit Bear

_____  9. This rock is carried up the hill and rolled down.

_____  10. "Until Peter _____ you, he won't heal."

_____  11. Their instincts were for life.

_____  12. Cole's wild laughter mocks the ingredients of his life's _____.

_____  13. a colorful, comforting blanket

_____  14. There is no place for this on the island.

_____  15. Cole takes and eats bits of this from the gulls.

_____  16. Cole destroys it with fire.

_____  17. Cole saves a handful of this but later discards it.

_____  18. Peter ruins and then fixes Cole's carving of this.

_____  19. provides food and a life lesson for Cole

_____  20. the lawyer hired by Cole's father

Touching Spirit Bear Fill in the Blank 1 Answer Key

| | | |
|---|---|---|
| ALONE | 1. | This state of being scares Cole more than anything else. |
| CHAMP | 2. | Garvey's nickname for Cole |
| CIRCLE | 3. | the last item carved on Cole's totem |
| MICE | 4. | They are often not noticed and see things others don't. |
| SUICIDE | 5. | Peter attempts this twice. |
| ROCK | 6. | becomes both ancestor and anger |
| FEATHER | 7. | symbolizes respect |
| MIKAELSEN | 8. | the author of Touching Spirit Bear |
| ANCESTOR | 9. | This rock is carried up the hill and rolled down. |
| FORGIVES | 10. | "Until Peter _____ you, he won't heal." |
| SPARROWS | 11. | Their instincts were for life. |
| CAKE | 12. | Cole's wild laughter mocks the ingredients of his life's _____. |
| AT.ÓOW | 13. | a colorful, comforting blanket |
| PRIDE | 14. | There is no place for this on the island. |
| FISH | 15. | Cole takes and eats bits of this from the gulls. |
| SHELTER | 16. | Cole destroys it with fire. |
| HAIR | 17. | Cole saves a handful of this but later discards it. |
| BEAR | 18. | Peter ruins and then fixes Cole's carving of this. |
| MOUSE | 19. | provides food and a life lesson for Cole |
| BLACKWOOD | 20. | the lawyer hired by Cole's father |

Touching Spirit Bear Fill in the Blank 2

_____ 1. They are often not noticed and see things others don't.

_____ 2. the morning ritual to clear Cole's mind

_____ 3. This rock is carried up the hill and rolled down.

_____ 4. "Whatever you do to the animals, you do to _____."

_____ 5. There is no place for this on the island.

_____ 6. "If you discover what's inside the _____, you'll discover what's inside of you."

_____ 7. It all looks the same to Cole.

_____ 8. Cole takes and eats bits of this from the gulls.

_____ 9. becomes both ancestor and anger

_____ 10. symbolizes respect

_____ 11. "Until Peter _____ you, he won't heal."

_____ 12. the person in charge of Circle Justice meetings

_____ 13. Peter ruins and then fixes Cole's carving of this.

_____ 14. Peter attempts this twice.

_____ 15. Cole does this at Edwin and the Spirit Bear.

_____ 16. It is a memory never forgotten.

_____ 17. Cole saves a handful of this but later discards it.

_____ 18. While recovering, Cole whispers, "My _____!"

_____ 19. Garvey's nickname for Cole

_____ 20. provides food and a life lesson for Cole

Touching Spirit Bear Fill in the Blank 2 Answer Key

| | |
|---|---|
| MICE | 1. They are often not noticed and see things others don't. |
| SOAK | 2. the morning ritual to clear Cole's mind |
| ANCESTOR | 3. This rock is carried up the hill and rolled down. |
| YOURSELF | 4. "Whatever you do to the animals, you do to _____." |
| PRIDE | 5. There is no place for this on the island. |
| WOOD | 6. "If you discover what's inside the _____, you'll discover what's inside of you." |
| BLOOD | 7. It all looks the same to Cole. |
| FISH | 8. Cole takes and eats bits of this from the gulls. |
| ROCK | 9. becomes both ancestor and anger |
| FEATHER | 10. symbolizes respect |
| FORGIVES | 11. "Until Peter _____ you, he won't heal." |
| KEEPER | 12. the person in charge of Circle Justice meetings |
| BEAR | 13. Peter ruins and then fixes Cole's carving of this. |
| SUICIDE | 14. Peter attempts this twice. |
| SPIT | 15. Cole does this at Edwin and the Spirit Bear. |
| ANGER | 16. It is a memory never forgotten. |
| HAIR | 17. Cole saves a handful of this but later discards it. |
| FAULT | 18. While recovering, Cole whispers, "My _____!" |
| CHAMP | 19. Garvey's nickname for Cole |
| MOUSE | 20. provides food and a life lesson for Cole |

Touching Spirit Bear Fill in the Blank 3

_____  1. provides food and a life lesson for Cole

_____  2. blames others for his life choices

_____  3. frequently performed as an expression of discovery

_____  4. the person in charge of Circle Justice meetings

_____  5. the animal that is graceful, powerful, and gentle

_____  6. becomes both ancestor and anger

_____  7. Cole's wild laughter mocks the ingredients of his life's _____.

_____  8. the victim of Cole's anger

_____  9. the morning ritual to clear Cole's mind

_____  10. tiny, infecting thistles: Devil's _____

_____  11. Garvey's nickname for Cole

_____  12. tells one's life story

_____  13. Cole saves a handful of this but later discards it.

_____  14. Cole describes his mom as a scared _____.

_____  15. Peter attempts this twice.

_____  16. To Cole, this is the adult term for passing the buck.

_____  17. This state of being scares Cole more than anything else.

_____  18. "If you discover what's inside the _____, you'll discover what's inside of you."
19. Their instincts were for life.

_____  20. While recovering, Cole whispers, "My _____!"

Touching Spirit Bear Fill in the Blank 3 Answer Key

| | |
|---|---|
| MOUSE | 1. provides food and a life lesson for Cole |
| COLE | 2. blames others for his life choices |
| DANCE | 3. frequently performed as an expression of discovery |
| KEEPER | 4. the person in charge of Circle Justice meetings |
| WHALE | 5. the animal that is graceful, powerful, and gentle |
| ROCK | 6. becomes both ancestor and anger |
| CAKE | 7. Cole's wild laughter mocks the ingredients of his life's _____. |
| PETER | 8. the victim of Cole's anger |
| SOAK | 9. the morning ritual to clear Cole's mind |
| CLUB | 10. tiny, infecting thistles: Devil's _____ |
| CHAMP | 11. Garvey's nickname for Cole |
| TOTEM | 12. tells one's life story |
| HAIR | 13. Cole saves a handful of this but later discards it. |
| BARBIE | 14. Cole describes his mom as a scared _____. |
| SUICIDE | 15. Peter attempts this twice. |
| REFERRED | 16. To Cole, this is the adult term for passing the buck. |
| ALONE | 17. This state of being scares Cole more than anything else. |
| WOOD | 18. "If you discover what's inside the _____, you'll discover what's inside of you." |
| SPARROWS | 19. Their instincts were for life. |
| FAULT | 20. While recovering, Cole whispers, "My _____!" |

Touching Spirit Bear Fill in the Blank 4

_____  1. Cole sleeps there during Peter's visit at first.

_____  2. frequently performed as an expression of discovery

_____  3. There is no place for this on the island.

_____  4. tiny, infecting thistles: Devil's _____

_____  5. nursed Cole right after his rescue

_____  6. symbolizes respect

_____  7. the person in charge of Circle Justice meetings

_____  8. The gulls pick at Cole's

_____  9. "If you discover what's inside the _____, you'll discover what's inside of you."

_____  10. It is a memory never forgotten.

_____  11. blames others for his life choices

_____  12. Mr. Matthews does not know Cole's _____.

_____  13. the victim of Cole's anger

_____  14. "Whatever you do to the animals, you do to _____."

_____  15. the last item carved on Cole's totem

_____  16. Cole saves a handful of this but later discards it.

_____  17. Cole connects with the Spirit Bear and feels this for the first time.

_____  18. the animal that is graceful, powerful, and gentle

_____  19. Cole destroys it with fire.

_____  20. an alcoholic child abuser

Touching Spirit Bear Fill in the Blank 4 Answer Key

| | |
|---|---|
| TENT | 1. Cole sleeps there during Peter's visit at first. |
| DANCE | 2. frequently performed as an expression of discovery |
| PRIDE | 3. There is no place for this on the island. |
| CLUB | 4. tiny, infecting thistles: Devil's _____ |
| ROSEY | 5. nursed Cole right after his rescue |
| FEATHER | 6. symbolizes respect |
| KEEPER | 7. the person in charge of Circle Justice meetings |
| FLESH | 8. The gulls pick at Cole's |
| WOOD | 9. "If you discover what's inside the _____, you'll discover what's inside of you." |
| ANGER | 10. It is a memory never forgotten. |
| COLE | 11. blames others for his life choices |
| BIRTHDAY | 12. Mr. Matthews does not know Cole's _____. |
| PETER | 13. the victim of Cole's anger |
| YOURSELF | 14. "Whatever you do to the animals, you do to _____." |
| CIRCLE | 15. the last item carved on Cole's totem |
| HAIR | 16. Cole saves a handful of this but later discards it. |
| TRUST | 17. Cole connects with the Spirit Bear and feels this for the first time. |
| WHALE | 18. the animal that is graceful, powerful, and gentle |
| SHELTER | 19. Cole destroys it with fire. |
| WILLIAM | 20. an alcoholic child abuser |

Touching Spirit Bear Matching 1

1. WOOD — A. Peter ruins and then fixes Cole's carving of this.
2. ALASKA — B. This rock is carried up the hill and rolled down.
3. PETER — C. provides food and a life lesson for Cole
4. DANCE — D. This state of being scares Cole more than anything else.
5. TENT — E. Mr. Matthews does not know Cole's _____.
6. COLE — F. Cole sleeps there during Peter's visit at first.
7. BLOOD — G. the victim of Cole's anger
8. SPIT — H. Cole is not afraid of this.
9. MOUSE — I. blames others for his life choices
10. DYING — J. Cole does this at Edwin and the Spirit Bear.
11. ALONE — K. the morning ritual to clear Cole's mind
12. WOLF — L. Edwin's native tribe
13. FISH — M. "If you discover what's inside the _____, you'll discover what's inside of you."
14. PRIDE — N. The _____ Bear mauls Cole.
15. BIRTHDAY — O. Circle _____ promotes healing.
16. YOURSELF — P. It all looks the same to Cole.
17. GARVEY — Q. nursed Cole right after his rescue
18. SPIRIT — R. All of life is like this.
19. HOTDOG — S. frequently performed as an expression of discovery
20. SOAK — T. "Whatever you do to the animals, you do to _____."
21. BEAR — U. There is no place for this on the island.
22. JUSTICE — V. Cole's parole officer
23. ANCESTOR — W. the location of the island
24. ROSEY — X. Cole takes and eats bits of this from the gulls.
25. TLINGIT — Y. the animal associated with the lesson "you need the help of others"

Touching Spirit Bear Matching 1 Answer Key

| | | | |
|---|---|---|---|
| M | 1. WOOD | A. | Peter ruins and then fixes Cole's carving of this. |
| W | 2. ALASKA | B. | This rock is carried up the hill and rolled down. |
| G | 3. PETER | C. | provides food and a life lesson for Cole |
| S | 4. DANCE | D. | This state of being scares Cole more than anything else. |
| F | 5. TENT | E. | Mr. Matthews does not know Cole's _____. |
| I | 6. COLE | F. | Cole sleeps there during Peter's visit at first. |
| P | 7. BLOOD | G. | the victim of Cole's anger |
| J | 8. SPIT | H. | Cole is not afraid of this. |
| C | 9. MOUSE | I. | blames others for his life choices |
| H | 10. DYING | J. | Cole does this at Edwin and the Spirit Bear. |
| D | 11. ALONE | K. | the morning ritual to clear Cole's mind |
| Y | 12. WOLF | L. | Edwin's native tribe |
| X | 13. FISH | M. | "If you discover what's inside the _____, you'll discover what's inside of you." |
| U | 14. PRIDE | N. | The _____ Bear mauls Cole. |
| E | 15. BIRTHDAY | O. | Circle _____ promotes healing. |
| T | 16. YOURSELF | P. | It all looks the same to Cole. |
| V | 17. GARVEY | Q. | nursed Cole right after his rescue |
| N | 18. SPIRIT | R. | All of life is like this. |
| R | 19. HOTDOG | S. | frequently performed as an expression of discovery |
| K | 20. SOAK | T. | "Whatever you do to the animals, you do to _____." |
| A | 21. BEAR | U. | There is no place for this on the island. |
| O | 22. JUSTICE | V. | Cole's parole officer |
| B | 23. ANCESTOR | W. | the location of the island |
| Q | 24. ROSEY | X. | Cole takes and eats bits of this from the gulls. |
| L | 25. TLINGIT | Y. | the animal associated with the lesson "you need the help of others" |

Touching Spirit Bear Matching 2

1. GARVEY — A. Cole sleeps there during Peter's visit at first.
2. EAGLE — B. the Tlingit Elder
3. TRUST — C. the person in charge of Circle Justice meetings
4. TOTEM — D. tells one's life story
5. BLOOD — E. nursed Cole right after his rescue
6. TENT — F. Cole connects with the Spirit Bear and feels this for the first time.
7. ANCESTOR — G. an instrument of destruction or healing
8. FEATHER — H. This rock is carried up the hill and rolled down.
9. AT.ÓOW — I. Cole describes his mom as a scared _____.
10. ROSEY — J. There is no place for this on the island.
11. PRIDE — K. a colorful, comforting blanket
12. WHALE — L. the author of Touching Spirit Bear
13. INVISIBLE — M. the animal associated with staying proud and viewing life differently from a distance
14. KNIFE — N. an alcoholic child abuser
15. BEAVER — O. the animal associated with lessons of persistence, patience, and ingenuity
16. MIKAELSEN — P. Cole wants to learn how to be this.
17. JUSTICE — Q. symbolizes respect
18. BIRTHDAY — R. It all looks the same to Cole.
19. WILLIAM — S. the animal that is graceful, powerful, and gentle
20. EDWIN — T. Mr. Matthews does not know Cole's _____.
21. BARBIE — U. Cole's parole officer
22. SWIM — V. Cole saves a handful of this but later discards it.
23. PETER — W. Cole's first method of attempted escape
24. HAIR — X. the victim of Cole's anger
25. KEEPER — Y. Circle _____ promotes healing.

Touching Spirit Bear Matching 2 Answer Key

| | | | |
|---|---|---|---|
| U | 1. GARVEY | A. | Cole sleeps there during Peter's visit at first. |
| M | 2. EAGLE | B. | the Tlingit Elder |
| F | 3. TRUST | C. | the person in charge of Circle Justice meetings |
| D | 4. TOTEM | D. | tells one's life story |
| R | 5. BLOOD | E. | nursed Cole right after his rescue |
| A | 6. TENT | F. | Cole connects with the Spirit Bear and feels this for the first time. |
| H | 7. ANCESTOR | G. | an instrument of destruction or healing |
| Q | 8. FEATHER | H. | This rock is carried up the hill and rolled down. |
| K | 9. AT.ÓOW | I. | Cole describes his mom as a scared _____. |
| E | 10. ROSEY | J. | There is no place for this on the island. |
| J | 11. PRIDE | K. | a colorful, comforting blanket |
| S | 12. WHALE | L. | the author of Touching Spirit Bear |
| P | 13. INVISIBLE | M. | the animal associated with staying proud and viewing life differently from a distance |
| G | 14. KNIFE | N. | an alcoholic child abuser |
| O | 15. BEAVER | O. | the animal associated with lessons of persistence, patience, and ingenuity |
| L | 16. MIKAELSEN | P. | Cole wants to learn how to be this. |
| Y | 17. JUSTICE | Q. | symbolizes respect |
| T | 18. BIRTHDAY | R. | It all looks the same to Cole. |
| N | 19. WILLIAM | S. | the animal that is graceful, powerful, and gentle |
| B | 20. EDWIN | T. | Mr. Matthews does not know Cole's _____. |
| I | 21. BARBIE | U. | Cole's parole officer |
| W | 22. SWIM | V. | Cole saves a handful of this but later discards it. |
| X | 23. PETER | W. | Cole's first method of attempted escape |
| V | 24. HAIR | X. | the victim of Cole's anger |
| C | 25. KEEPER | Y. | Circle _____ promotes healing. |

Touching Spirit Bear Matching 3

1. SHELTER  A. the person in charge of Circle Justice meetings
2. TLINGIT  B. "Until Peter _____ you, he won't heal."
3. ALONE  C. There is no place for this on the island.
4. KEEPER  D. Cole wants to learn how to be this.
5. JUSTICE  E. Circle _____ promotes healing.
6. COLE  F. Cole describes his mom as a scared _____.
7. FORGIVES  G. Their instincts were for life.
8. CAKE  H. the last item carved on Cole's totem
9. FAULT  I. Cole does this at Edwin and the Spirit Bear.
10. TOTEM  J. the morning ritual to clear Cole's mind
11. GARVEY  K. the location of the island
12. BIRTHDAY  L. blames others for his life choices
13. PRIDE  M. Cole destroys it with fire.
14. INVISIBLE  N. Garvey's nickname for Cole
15. CHAMP  O. Mr. Matthews does not know Cole's _____.
16. SPARROWS  P. Cole's wild laughter mocks the ingredients of his life's _____.
17. MOUSE  Q. "If you discover what's inside the _____, you'll discover what's inside of you."
18. BARBIE  R. the lawyer hired by Cole's father
19. SPIT  S. To Cole, this is the adult term for passing the buck.
20. SOAK  T. While recovering, Cole whispers, "My _____!"
21. ALASKA  U. tells one's life story
22. CIRCLE  V. provides food and a life lesson for Cole
23. WOOD  W. This state of being scares Cole more than anything else.
24. REFERRED  X. Cole's parole officer
25. BLACKWOOD  Y. Edwin's native tribe

Touching Spirit Bear Matching 3 Answer Key

| | | | | |
|---|---|---|---|---|
| M | 1. SHELTER | | A. | the person in charge of Circle Justice meetings |
| Y | 2. TLINGIT | | B. | "Until Peter _____ you, he won't heal." |
| W | 3. ALONE | | C. | There is no place for this on the island. |
| A | 4. KEEPER | | D. | Cole wants to learn how to be this. |
| E | 5. JUSTICE | | E. | Circle _____ promotes healing. |
| L | 6. COLE | | F. | Cole describes his mom as a scared _____. |
| B | 7. FORGIVES | | G. | Their instincts were for life. |
| P | 8. CAKE | | H. | the last item carved on Cole's totem |
| T | 9. FAULT | | I. | Cole does this at Edwin and the Spirit Bear. |
| U | 10. TOTEM | | J. | the morning ritual to clear Cole's mind |
| X | 11. GARVEY | | K. | the location of the island |
| O | 12. BIRTHDAY | | L. | blames others for his life choices |
| C | 13. PRIDE | | M. | Cole destroys it with fire. |
| D | 14. INVISIBLE | | N. | Garvey's nickname for Cole |
| N | 15. CHAMP | | O. | Mr. Matthews does not know Cole's _____. |
| G | 16. SPARROWS | | P. | Cole's wild laughter mocks the ingredients of his life's _____. |
| V | 17. MOUSE | | Q. | "If you discover what's inside the _____, you'll discover what's inside of you." |
| F | 18. BARBIE | | R. | the lawyer hired by Cole's father |
| I | 19. SPIT | | S. | To Cole, this is the adult term for passing the buck. |
| J | 20. SOAK | | T. | While recovering, Cole whispers, "My _____!" |
| K | 21. ALASKA | | U. | tells one's life story |
| H | 22. CIRCLE | | V. | provides food and a life lesson for Cole |
| Q | 23. WOOD | | W. | This state of being scares Cole more than anything else. |
| S | 24. REFERRED | | X. | Cole's parole officer |
| R | 25. BLACKWOOD | | Y. | Edwin's native tribe |

# Touching Spirit Bear Matching 4

1. TLINGIT
2. PETER
3. SPIT
4. SWIM
5. CAKE
6. BIRTHDAY
7. CHAMP
8. KNIFE
9. SPARROWS
10. WHALE
11. INVISIBLE
12. WILLIAM
13. SPIRIT
14. BLOOD
15. BARBIE
16. REFERRED
17. SUICIDE
18. SOAK
19. DYING
20. PRIDE
21. WOLF
22. COLE
23. FISH
24. ALASKA
25. DANCE

A. Their instincts were for life.
B. frequently performed as an expression of discovery
C. Cole is not afraid of this.
D. Peter attempts this twice.
E. Mr. Matthews does not know Cole's _____.
F. There is no place for this on the island.
G. Garvey's nickname for Cole
H. Cole does this at Edwin and the Spirit Bear.
I. Edwin's native tribe
J. blames others for his life choices
K. Cole's first method of attempted escape
L. an instrument of destruction or healing
M. Cole takes and eats bits of this from the gulls.
N. the location of the island
O. The _____ Bear mauls Cole.
P. an alcoholic child abuser
Q. Cole describes his mom as a scared _____.
R. It all looks the same to Cole.
S. the animal associated with the lesson "you need the help of others"
T. the morning ritual to clear Cole's mind
U. Cole's wild laughter mocks the ingredients of his life's _____.
V. Cole wants to learn how to be this.
W. To Cole, this is the adult term for passing the buck.
X. the animal that is graceful, powerful, and gentle
Y. the victim of Cole's anger

Touching Spirit Bear Matching 4 Answer Key

| | | | |
|---|---|---|---|
| I | 1. TLINGIT | A. | Their instincts were for life. |
| Y | 2. PETER | B. | frequently performed as an expression of discovery |
| H | 3. SPIT | C. | Cole is not afraid of this. |
| K | 4. SWIM | D. | Peter attempts this twice. |
| U | 5. CAKE | E. | Mr. Matthews does not know Cole's _____. |
| E | 6. BIRTHDAY | F. | There is no place for this on the island. |
| G | 7. CHAMP | G. | Garvey's nickname for Cole |
| L | 8. KNIFE | H. | Cole does this at Edwin and the Spirit Bear. |
| A | 9. SPARROWS | I. | Edwin's native tribe |
| X | 10. WHALE | J. | blames others for his life choices |
| V | 11. INVISIBLE | K. | Cole's first method of attempted escape |
| P | 12. WILLIAM | L. | an instrument of destruction or healing |
| O | 13. SPIRIT | M. | Cole takes and eats bits of this from the gulls. |
| R | 14. BLOOD | N. | the location of the island |
| Q | 15. BARBIE | O. | The _____ Bear mauls Cole. |
| W | 16. REFERRED | P. | an alcoholic child abuser |
| D | 17. SUICIDE | Q. | Cole describes his mom as a scared _____. |
| T | 18. SOAK | R. | It all looks the same to Cole. |
| C | 19. DYING | S. | the animal associated with the lesson "you need the help of others" |
| F | 20. PRIDE | T. | the morning ritual to clear Cole's mind |
| S | 21. WOLF | U. | Cole's wild laughter mocks the ingredients of his life's _____. |
| J | 22. COLE | V. | Cole wants to learn how to be this. |
| M | 23. FISH | W. | To Cole, this is the adult term for passing the buck. |
| N | 24. ALASKA | X. | the animal that is graceful, powerful, and gentle |
| B | 25. DANCE | Y. | the victim of Cole's anger |

Touching Spirit Bear Magic Squares 1

Match the definition with the vocabulary word. Put your answers in the magic squares below. When your answers are correct, all columns and rows will add to the same number.

A. FEATHER
B. BEAR
C. FORGIVES
D. DYING

E. MIKAELSEN
F. ROSEY
G. ROCK
H. ANGER

I. SUPPER
J. PETER
K. FLESH
L. EAGLE

M. MICE
N. INVISIBLE
O. TLINGIT
P. WHALE

1. They are often not noticed and see things others don't.
2. nursed Cole right after his rescue
3. It is a memory never forgotten.
4. Edwin's native tribe
5. the animal associated with staying proud and viewing life differently from a distance
6. "Until Peter _____ you, he won't heal."
7. symbolizes respect
8. the victim of Cole's anger
9. The gulls pick at Cole's
10. Cole is not afraid of this.
11. Peter ruins and then fixes Cole's carving of this.
12. "It's not about _____...You're still...looking for the easiest way to get by."
13. Cole wants to learn how to be this.
14. the author of Touching Spirit Bear
15. becomes both ancestor and anger
16. the animal that is graceful, powerful, and gentle

| A= | B= | C= | D= |
| E= | F= | G= | H= |
| I= | J= | K= | L= |
| M= | N= | O= | P= |

Touching Spirit Bear Magic Squares 1 Answer Key

Match the definition with the vocabulary word. Put your answers in the magic squares below. When your answers are correct, all columns and rows will add to the same number.

A. FEATHER
B. BEAR
C. FORGIVES
D. DYING
E. MIKAELSEN
F. ROSEY
G. ROCK
H. ANGER
I. SUPPER
J. PETER
K. FLESH
L. EAGLE
M. MICE
N. INVISIBLE
O. TLINGIT
P. WHALE

1. They are often not noticed and see things others don't.
2. nursed Cole right after his rescue
3. It is a memory never forgotten.
4. Edwin's native tribe
5. the animal associated with staying proud and viewing life differently from a distance
6. "Until Peter _____ you, he won't heal."
7. symbolizes respect
8. the victim of Cole's anger
9. The gulls pick at Cole's
10. Cole is not afraid of this.
11. Peter ruins and then fixes Cole's carving of this.
12. "It's not about _____...You're still...looking for the easiest way to get by."
13. Cole wants to learn how to be this.
14. the author of Touching Spirit Bear
15. becomes both ancestor and anger
16. the animal that is graceful, powerful, and gentle

| A=7 | B=11 | C=6 | D=10 |
|---|---|---|---|
| E=14 | F=2 | G=15 | H=3 |
| I=12 | J=8 | K=9 | L=5 |
| M=1 | N=13 | O=4 | P=16 |

Touching Spirit Bear Magic Squares 2

Match the definition with the vocabulary word. Put your answers in the magic squares below. When your answers are correct, all columns and rows will add to the same number.

A. ANCESTOR
B. REFERRED
C. FAULT
D. CHAMP
E. HOTDOG
F. WOOD
G. ALASKA
H. MICE
I. SHELTER
J. BEAR
K. SPARROWS
L. TENT
M. COLE
N. EDWIN
O. SWIM
P. WOLF

1. "If you discover what's inside the _____, you'll discover what's inside of you."
2. Cole destroys it with fire.
3. Cole's first method of attempted escape
4. Garvey's nickname for Cole
5. blames others for his life choices
6. To Cole, this is the adult term for passing the buck.
7. They are often not noticed and see things others don't.
8. Their instincts were for life.
9. While recovering, Cole whispers, "My _____, _____!"
10. the animal associated with the lesson "you need the help of others"
11. Peter ruins and then fixes Cole's carving of this.
12. All of life is like this.
13. Cole sleeps there during Peter's visit at first.
14. the location of the island
15. This rock is carried up the hill and rolled down.
16. the Tlingit Elder

| A= | B= | C= | D= |
| E= | F= | G= | H= |
| I= | J= | K= | L= |
| M= | N= | O= | P= |

Touching Spirit Bear Magic Squares 2 Answer Key

Match the definition with the vocabulary word. Put your answers in the magic squares below. When your answers are correct, all columns and rows will add to the same number.

A. ANCESTOR
B. REFERRED
C. FAULT
D. CHAMP
E. HOTDOG
F. WOOD
G. ALASKA
H. MICE
I. SHELTER
J. BEAR
K. SPARROWS
L. TENT
M. COLE
N. EDWIN
O. SWIM
P. WOLF

1. "If you discover what's inside the _____, _____!" you'll discover what's inside of you."
2. Cole destroys it with fire.
3. Cole's first method of attempted escape
4. Garvey's nickname for Cole
5. blames others for his life choices
6. To Cole, this is the adult term for passing the buck.
7. They are often not noticed and see things others don't.
8. Their instincts were for life.
9. While recovering, Cole whispers, "My
10. the animal associated with the lesson "you need the help of others"
11. Peter ruins and then fixes Cole's carving of this.
12. All of life is like this.
13. Cole sleeps there during Peter's visit at first.
14. the location of the island
15. This rock is carried up the hill and rolled down.
16. the Tlingit Elder

| A=15 | B=6 | C=9 | D=4 |
| E=12 | F=1 | G=14 | H=7 |
| I=2 | J=11 | K=8 | L=13 |
| M=5 | N=16 | O=3 | P=10 |

Touching Spirit Bear Magic Squares 3

Match the definition with the vocabulary word. Put your answers in the magic squares below. When your answers are correct, all columns and rows will add to the same number.

A. BEAR
B. ALASKA
C. CLUB
D. SUICIDE
E. ROCK
F. SPARROWS
G. BEAVER
H. PETER
I. TRUST
J. WOOD
K. YOURSELF
L. CIRCLE
M. BIRTHDAY
N. SWIM
O. BLOOD
P. MIKAELSEN

1. It all looks the same to Cole.
2. Peter attempts this twice.
3. "If you discover what's inside the _____, you'll discover what's inside of you."
4. becomes both ancestor and anger
5. Cole connects with the Spirit Bear and feels this for the first time.
6. Their instincts were for life.
7. the author of Touching Spirit Bear
8. tiny, infecting thistles: Devil's _____
9. the victim of Cole's anger
10. "Whatever you do to the animals, you do to _____."
11. Peter ruins and then fixes Cole's carving of this.
12. Cole's first method of attempted escape
13. the location of the island
14. Mr. Matthews does not know Cole's _____.
15. the animal associated with lessons of persistence, patience, and ingenuity
16. the last item carved on Cole's totem

| A= | B= | C= | D= |
| --- | --- | --- | --- |
| E= | F= | G= | H= |
| I= | J= | K= | L= |
| M= | N= | O= | P= |

Touching Spirit Bear Magic Squares 3 Answer Key

Match the definition with the vocabulary word. Put your answers in the magic squares below. When your answers are correct, all columns and rows will add to the same number.

A. BEAR
B. ALASKA
C. CLUB
D. SUICIDE
E. ROCK
F. SPARROWS
G. BEAVER
H. PETER
I. TRUST
J. WOOD
K. YOURSELF
L. CIRCLE
M. BIRTHDAY
N. SWIM
O. BLOOD
P. MIKAELSEN

1. It all looks the same to Cole.
2. Peter attempts this twice.
3. "If you discover what's inside the _____, you'll discover what's inside of you."
4. becomes both ancestor and anger
5. Cole connects with the Spirit Bear and feels this for the first time.
6. Their instincts were for life.
7. the author of Touching Spirit Bear
8. tiny, infecting thistles: Devil's _____
9. the victim of Cole's anger
10. "Whatever you do to the animals, you do to _____."
11. Peter ruins and then fixes Cole's carving of this.
12. Cole's first method of attempted escape
13. the location of the island
14. Mr. Matthews does not know Cole's _____.
15. the animal associated with lessons of persistence, patience, and ingenuity
16. the last item carved on Cole's totem

| A=11 | B=13 | C=8 | D=2 |
| --- | --- | --- | --- |
| E=4 | F=6 | G=15 | H=9 |
| I=5 | J=3 | K=10 | L=16 |
| M=14 | N=12 | O=1 | P=7 |

Touching Spirit Bear Magic Squares 4

Match the definition with the vocabulary word. Put your answers in the magic squares below. When your answers are correct, all columns and rows will add to the same number.

A. FAULT
B. HOTDOG
C. BEAVER
D. FORGIVES
E. WOOD
F. YOURSELF
G. BARBIE
H. ROSEY
I. SHELTER
J. SUICIDE
K. HAIR
L. MICE
M. KEEPER
N. JUSTICE
O. BLOOD
P. TLINGIT

1. nursed Cole right after his rescue
2. the person in charge of Circle Justice meetings
3. All of life is like this.
4. Cole saves a handful of this but later discards it.
5. Peter attempts this twice.
6. the animal associated with lessons of persistence, patience, and ingenuity
7. Edwin's native tribe
8. "If you discover what's inside the _____, you'll discover what's inside of you."
9. It all looks the same to Cole.
10. "Whatever you do to the animals, you do to _____."
11. Cole destroys it with fire.
12. "Until Peter _____ you, he won't heal."
13. While recovering, Cole whispers, "My _____!"
14. They are often not noticed and see things others don't.
15. Cole describes his mom as a scared _____.
16. Circle _____ promotes healing.

| A= | B= | C= | D= |
| E= | F= | G= | H= |
| I= | J= | K= | L= |
| M= | N= | O= | P= |

Touching Spirit Bear Magic Squares 4 Answer Key

Match the definition with the vocabulary word. Put your answers in the magic squares below. When your answers are correct, all columns and rows will add to the same number.

A. FAULT
B. HOTDOG
C. BEAVER
D. FORGIVES
E. WOOD
F. YOURSELF
G. BARBIE
H. ROSEY
I. SHELTER
J. SUICIDE
K. HAIR
L. MICE
M. KEEPER
N. JUSTICE
O. BLOOD
P. TLINGIT

1. nursed Cole right after his rescue
2. the person in charge of Circle Justice meetings
3. All of life is like this.
4. Cole saves a handful of this but later discards it.
5. Peter attempts this twice.
6. the animal associated with lessons of persistence, patience, and ingenuity
7. Edwin's native tribe
8. "If you discover what's inside the _____, you'll discover what's inside of you."
9. It all looks the same to Cole.
10. "Whatever you do to the animals, you do to _____."
11. Cole destroys it with fire.
12. "Until Peter _____ you, he won't heal."
13. While recovering, Cole whispers, "My _____!"
14. They are often not noticed and see things others don't.
15. Cole describes his mom as a scared _____.
16. Circle _____ promotes healing.

| A=13 | B=3 | C=6 | D=12 |
| E=8 | F=10 | G=15 | H=1 |
| I=11 | J=5 | K=4 | L=14 |
| M=2 | N=16 | O=9 | P=7 |

# Touching Spirit Bear Word Search 1

Words are placed backwards, forward, diagonally, up and down. Clues listed below can help you find the words. Circle the hidden vocabulary words in the maze.

```
W C G K R S R R F B W W D G B
M I N N E A P O L I S O O N X
Y R P C L B R T C N S D O L P
F C J R B G E S D K T H L D F
N L A U I T G E K O B Y B K P
B E Z V S R N C H S U P P E R
B A E U I T A N O C L W S E E
D S R A V L I A Q H C U P P T
T T H B N V K C R A O S Y E E
T W E T I T O T E M E D I R P
I H D K S E E K Z P F X S O G
R A W A J C A N S P I T W S M
I L I G N C O H T Z N J I E I
P E N B N C A L A S K A M Y C
S U I C I D E F E N O L A G E
```

"If you discover what's inside the _____, you'll discover what's inside of you." (4)
"It's not about _____...You're still...looking for the easiest way to get by." (6)
"Until Peter _____ you, he won't heal." (8)
All of life is like this. (6)
Circle _____ promotes healing. (7)
Cole connects with the Spirit Bear and feels this for the first time. (5)
Cole describes his mom as a scared _____. (6)
Cole does this at Edwin and the Spirit Bear. (4)
Cole saves a handful of this but later discards it. (4)
Cole sleeps there during Peter's visit at first. (4)
Cole takes and eats bits of this from the gulls. (4)
Cole wants to learn how to be this. (9)
Cole's first method of attempted escape (4)
Cole's wild laughter mocks the ingredients of his life's _____. (4)
Garvey's nickname for Cole (5)
It all looks the same to Cole. (5)
It is a memory never forgotten. (5)
Peter attempts this twice. (7)
Peter ruins and then fixes Cole's carving of this. (4)
The _____ Bear mauls Cole. (6)
There is no place for this on the island. (5)

They are often not noticed and see things others don't. (4)
This rock is carried up the hill and rolled down. (8)
This state of being scares Cole more than anything else. (5)
an instrument of destruction or healing (5)
becomes both ancestor and anger (4)
blames others for his life choices (4)
frequently performed as an expression of discovery (5)
nursed Cole right after his rescue (5)
provides food and a life lesson for Cole (5)
tells one's life story (5)
the Tlingit Elder (5)
the animal associated with the lesson "you need the help of others" (4)
the animal that is graceful, powerful, and gentle (5)
the hometown of the Matthews family (11)
the last item carved on Cole's totem (6)
the location of the island (6)
the morning ritual to clear Cole's mind (4)
the person in charge of Circle Justice meetings (6)
the victim of Cole's anger (5)
tiny, infecting thistles: Devil's _____ (4)

Touching Spirit Bear Word Search 1 Answer Key

Words are placed backwards, forward, diagonally, up and down. Clues listed below can help you find the words. Circle the hidden vocabulary words in the maze.

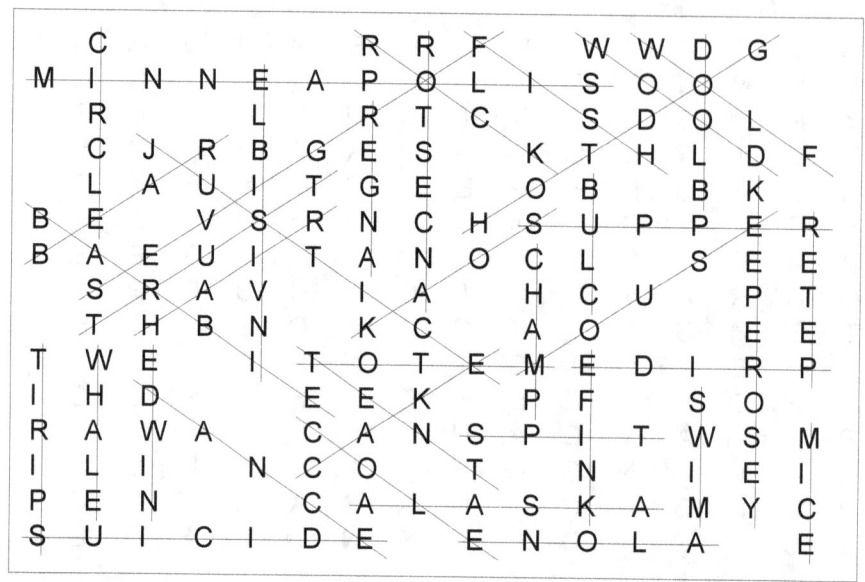

"If you discover what's inside the _____, you'll discover what's inside of you." (4)
"It's not about _____...You're still...looking for the easiest way to get by." (6)
"Until Peter _____ you, he won't heal." (8)
All of life is like this. (6)
Circle _____ promotes healing. (7)
Cole connects with the Spirit Bear and feels this for the first time. (5)
Cole describes his mom as a scared _____. (6)
Cole does this at Edwin and the Spirit Bear. (4)
Cole saves a handful of this but later discards it. (4)
Cole sleeps there during Peter's visit at first. (4)
Cole takes and eats bits of this from the gulls. (4)
Cole wants to learn how to be this. (9)
Cole's first method of attempted escape (4)
Cole's wild laughter mocks the ingredients of his life's _____. (4)
Garvey's nickname for Cole (5)
It all looks the same to Cole. (5)
It is a memory never forgotten. (5)
Peter attempts this twice. (7)
Peter ruins and then fixes Cole's carving of this. (4)
The _____ Bear mauls Cole. (6)
There is no place for this on the island. (5)

They are often not noticed and see things others don't. (4)
This rock is carried up the hill and rolled down. (8)
This state of being scares Cole more than anything else. (5)
an instrument of destruction or healing (5)
becomes both ancestor and anger (4)
blames others for his life choices (4)
frequently performed as an expression of discovery (5)
nursed Cole right after his rescue (5)
provides food and a life lesson for Cole (5)
tells one's life story (5)
the Tlingit Elder (5)
the animal associated with the lesson "you need the help of others" (4)
the animal that is graceful, powerful, and gentle (5)
the hometown of the Matthews family (11)
the last item carved on Cole's totem (6)
the location of the island (6)
the morning ritual to clear Cole's mind (4)
the person in charge of Circle Justice meetings (6)
the victim of Cole's anger (5)
tiny, infecting thistles: Devil's _____ (4)

Touching Spirit Bear Word Search 2

Words are placed backwards, forward, diagonally, up and down. Clues listed below can help you find the words. Circle the hidden vocabulary words in the maze.

```
F Y C S H E L T E R A R P B S
C I O E C N A D N G F N O Z O
Z H S U W A S G O L A L G C A
W G A H R I T W L A U W E E K
G O S M M S L . A E L S O S R
T A O E P S E L O B T A P L H
B L R D D M U L I O A O S I F
F E I V T W M P F A W R T K T
E C A N E D I R P J M E B E A
A J W V G Y C N U E F D P I M
T X C W E I E S P I R I T T E
H G T H L R T H N O S K B S C
E G E A O I A K S D W R U U A
R F N L C I L E M B I O L R K
P E T E R D Y I N G M D C T E
```

"If you discover what's inside the _____, you'll discover what's inside of you." (4)
"It's not about _____...You're still...looking for the easiest way to get by." (6)
"Whatever you do to the animals, you do to _____." (8)
Circle _____ promotes healing. (7)
Cole connects with the Spirit Bear and feels this for the first time. (5)
Cole describes his mom as a scared _____. (6)
Cole destroys it with fire. (7)
Cole does this at Edwin and the Spirit Bear. (4)
Cole is not afraid of this. (5)
Cole saves a handful of this but later discards it. (4)
Cole sleeps there during Peter's visit at first. (4)
Cole takes and eats bits of this from the gulls. (4)
Cole's first method of attempted escape (4)
Cole's parole officer (6)
Cole's wild laughter mocks the ingredients of his life's _____. (4)
Edwin's native tribe (7)
Garvey's nickname for Cole (5)
It is a memory never forgotten. (5)
The _____ Bear mauls Cole. (6)
The gulls pick at Cole's (5)
There is no place for this on the island. (5)
They are often not noticed and see things others don't. (4)
This state of being scares Cole more than anything else. (5)
While recovering, Cole whispers, "My _____!" (5)
a colorful, comforting blanket (6)
an alcoholic child abuser (7)
an instrument of destruction or healing (5)
becomes both ancestor and anger (4)
blames others for his life choices (4)
frequently performed as an expression of discovery (5)
nursed Cole right after his rescue (5)
provides food and a life lesson for Cole (5)
symbolizes respect (7)
tells one's life story (5)
the Tlingit Elder (5)
the animal associated with lessons of persistence, patience, and ingenuity (6)
the animal associated with staying proud and viewing life differently from a distance (5)
the animal associated with the lesson "you need the help of others" (4)
the animal that is graceful, powerful, and gentle (5)
the location of the island (6)
the morning ritual to clear Cole's mind (4)
the victim of Cole's anger (5)
tiny, infecting thistles: Devil's _____ (4)

Touching Spirit Bear Word Search 2 Answer Key

Words are placed backwards, forward, diagonally, up and down. Clues listed below can help you find the words. Circle the hidden vocabulary words in the maze.

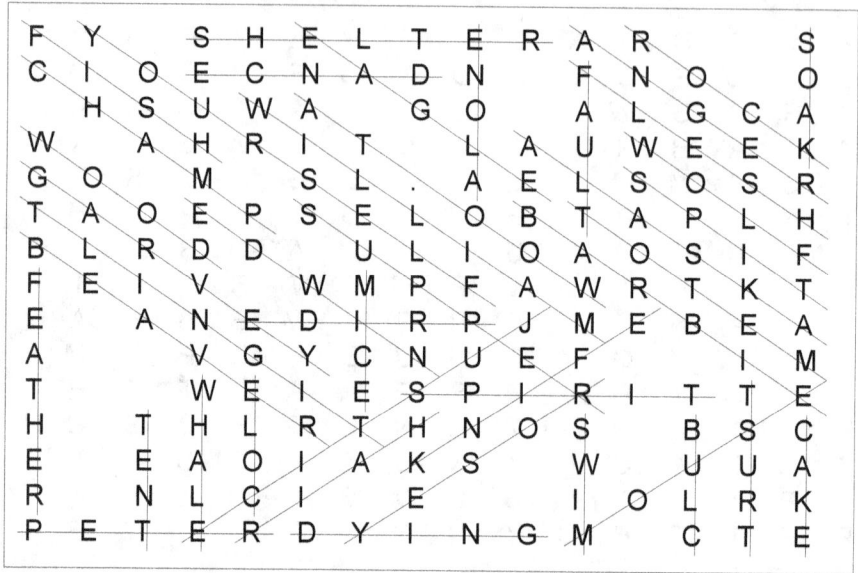

"If you discover what's inside the _____, you'll discover what's inside of you." (4)
"It's not about _____...You're still...looking for the easiest way to get by." (6)
"Whatever you do to the animals, you do to _____." (8)
Circle _____ promotes healing. (7)
Cole connects with the Spirit Bear and feels this for the first time. (5)
Cole describes his mom as a scared _____. (6)
Cole destroys it with fire. (7)
Cole does this at Edwin and the Spirit Bear. (4)
Cole is not afraid of this. (5)
Cole saves a handful of this but later discards it. (4)
Cole sleeps there during Peter's visit at first. (4)
Cole takes and eats bits of this from the gulls. (4)
Cole's first method of attempted escape (4)
Cole's parole officer (6)
Cole's wild laughter mocks the ingredients of his life's _____. (4)
Edwin's native tribe (7)
Garvey's nickname for Cole (5)
It is a memory never forgotten. (5)
The _____ Bear mauls Cole. (6)
The gulls pick at Cole's (5)
There is no place for this on the island. (5)
They are often not noticed and see things others don't. (4)
This state of being scares Cole more than anything else. (5)
While recovering, Cole whispers, "My _____!" (5)
a colorful, comforting blanket (6)
an alcoholic child abuser (7)
an instrument of destruction or healing (5)
becomes both ancestor and anger (4)
blames others for his life choices (4)
frequently performed as an expression of discovery (5)
nursed Cole right after his rescue (5)
provides food and a life lesson for Cole (5)
symbolizes respect (7)
tells one's life story (5)
the Tlingit Elder (5)
the animal associated with lessons of persistence, patience, and ingenuity (6)
the animal associated with staying proud and viewing life differently from a distance (5)
the animal associated with the lesson "you need the help of others" (4)
the animal that is graceful, powerful, and gentle (5)
the location of the island (6)
the morning ritual to clear Cole's mind (4)
the victim of Cole's anger (5)
tiny, infecting thistles: Devil's _____ (4)

# Touching Spirit Bear Word Search 3

Words are placed backwards, forward, diagonally, up and down. Words listed below are included in the maze. Circle the hidden vocabulary words in the maze.

```
W T C H A M P W C R E X G W F
O R O K N I F E O S D S R I E
O Q Y T C R C Y U L C O X L A
D A N C E B L O O D F A U L T
N B L P S M M U L B I K N I H
Q U E R T J Y R S E S M P A E
B E N A O N V S S F H S S M R
K D O X R C H E D W U W U I J
S W L X E E K L C P I T I K U
P I A K L W N F P R E M C A S
I N A T O E L E I N A A I E T
R C E O C E R A T Y G N D L I
I R . I S W H A L E L G E S C
T T M H A L A S K A E E C E E
A T L I N G I T E D I R P N J
```

| | | | |
|---|---|---|---|
| ALASKA | DANCE | MICE | SWIM |
| ALONE | EAGLE | MIKAELSEN | TENT |
| ANCESTOR | EDWIN | MOUSE | TLINGIT |
| ANGER | FAULT | PRIDE | TOTEM |
| AT.OOW | FEATHER | ROCK | WHALE |
| BEAR | FISH | SHELTER | WILLIAM |
| BLOOD | FLESH | SOAK | WOLF |
| CAKE | HAIR | SPIRIT | WOOD |
| CHAMP | JUSTICE | SPIT | YOURSELF |
| CLUB | KEEPER | SUICIDE | |
| COLE | KNIFE | SUPPER | |

Touching Spirit Bear Word Search 3 Answer Key

Words are placed backwards, forward, diagonally, up and down. Words listed below are included in the maze. Circle the hidden vocabulary words in the maze.

| ALASKA | DANCE | MICE | SWIM |
| ALONE | EAGLE | MIKAELSEN | TENT |
| ANCESTOR | EDWIN | MOUSE | TLINGIT |
| ANGER | FAULT | PRIDE | TOTEM |
| AT.OOW | FEATHER | ROCK | WHALE |
| BEAR | FISH | SHELTER | WILLIAM |
| BLOOD | FLESH | SOAK | WOLF |
| CAKE | HAIR | SPIRIT | WOOD |
| CHAMP | JUSTICE | SPIT | YOURSELF |
| CLUB | KEEPER | SUICIDE | |
| COLE | KNIFE | SUPPER | |

Touching Spirit Bear Word Search 4

Words are placed backwards, forward, diagonally, up and down. Words listed below are included in the maze. Circle the hidden vocabulary words in the maze.

```
W H A L E D I C I U S W O L F
B X H E A B G F J U S T I C E
U Q K V N L J L N Y W R K T K
L A N G E R A E E X H O C A R
C G A R V E Y S P A R R O W S
A H M D D B O H K H E S R D R
N W A O A R M T A A T H R D F
C B I M U N I O L T L T A Y T
E K L L P S C T O R E H S I F
S D N O L W E E N U H L P N R
T P W I O I F M E S S S I G E
O S R I F D A Y H T T F R C P
R L W I N E U M T N W Z I O P
T B L I D W L P E T E R T L U
B E A R M E T T E A G L E E S
```

| | | | |
|---|---|---|---|
| ALASKA | DYING | MOUSE | SUPPER |
| ALONE | EAGLE | PETER | SWIM |
| ANCESTOR | EDWIN | PRIDE | TENT |
| ANGER | FAULT | ROCK | TOTEM |
| BEAR | FISH | ROSEY | TRUST |
| BLOOD | FLESH | SHELTER | WHALE |
| CAKE | GARVEY | SOAK | WILLIAM |
| CHAMP | HAIR | SPARROWS | WOLF |
| CLUB | JUSTICE | SPIRIT | WOOD |
| COLE | KNIFE | SPIT | |
| DANCE | MICE | SUICIDE | |

Touching Spirit Bear Word Search 4 Answer Key

Words are placed backwards, forward, diagonally, up and down. Words listed below are included in the maze. Circle the hidden vocabulary words in the maze.

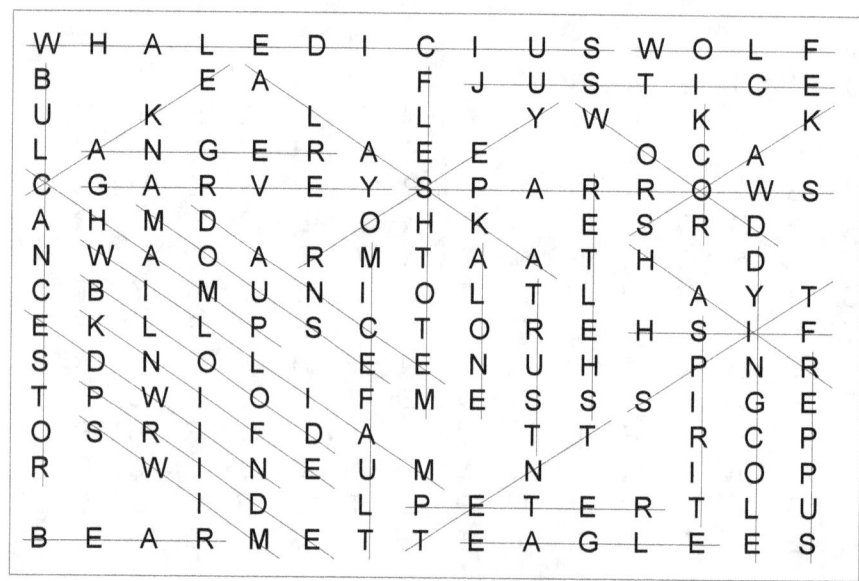

| ALASKA | DYING | MOUSE | SUPPER |
| ALONE | EAGLE | PETER | SWIM |
| ANCESTOR | EDWIN | PRIDE | TENT |
| ANGER | FAULT | ROCK | TOTEM |
| BEAR | FISH | ROSEY | TRUST |
| BLOOD | FLESH | SHELTER | WHALE |
| CAKE | GARVEY | SOAK | WILLIAM |
| CHAMP | HAIR | SPARROWS | WOLF |
| CLUB | JUSTICE | SPIRIT | WOOD |
| COLE | KNIFE | SPIT | |
| DANCE | MICE | SUICIDE | |

Touching Spirit Bear Crossword 1

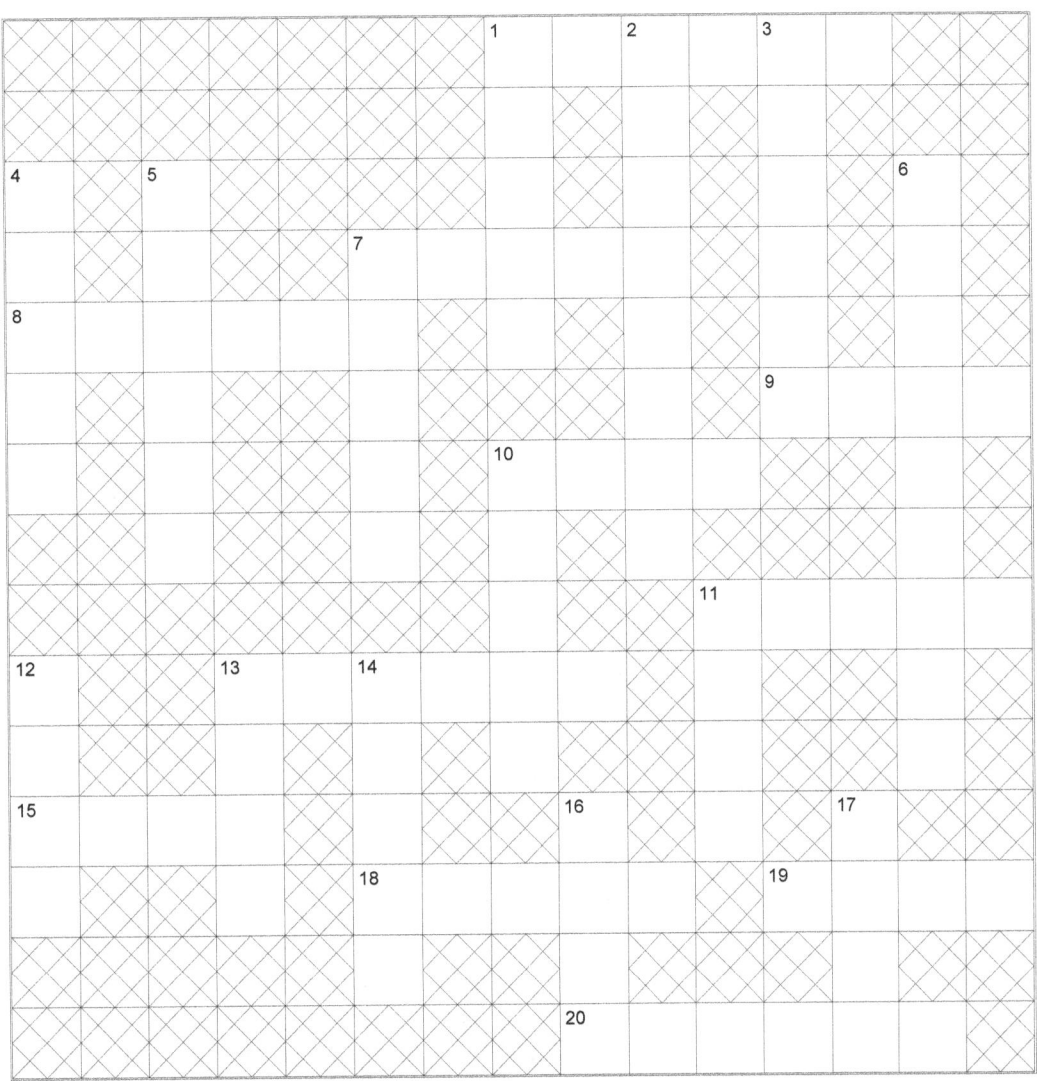

Across
1. the location of the island
7. frequently performed as an expression of discovery
8. Cole's parole officer
9. becomes both ancestor and anger
10. "If you discover what's inside the _____, you'll discover what's inside of you."
11. It all looks the same to Cole.
13. the last item carved on Cole's totem
15. the morning ritual to clear Cole's mind
18. the animal associated with staying proud and viewing life differently from a distance
19. the animal associated with the lesson "you need the help of others"
20. the animal associated with lessons of persistence, patience, and ingenuity

Down
1. This state of being scares Cole more than anything else.
2. This rock is carried up the hill and rolled down.
3. the person in charge of Circle Justice meetings
4. It is a memory never forgotten.
5. Cole describes his mom as a scared _____.
6. the lawyer hired by Cole's father
7. Cole is not afraid of this.
10. the animal that is graceful, powerful, and gentle
11. Peter ruins and then fixes Cole's carving of this.
12. Cole takes and eats bits of this from the gulls.
13. Cole's wild laughter mocks the ingredients of his life's _____.
14. nursed Cole right after his rescue
16. tiny, infecting thistles: Devil's _____
17. blames others for his life choices

Touching Spirit Bear Crossword 1 Answer Key

|   |   |   |   |   |   | ¹A | L | ²A | S | ³K | A |   |
|---|---|---|---|---|---|---|---|---|---|---|---|---|
|   |   |   |   |   |   | L |   | N |   | E |   |   |
| ⁴A |   | ⁵B |   |   |   | O |   | C |   | E |   | ⁶B |
| N |   | A |   |   | ⁷D | A | N | C | E |   |   | L |
| ⁸G | A | R | V | E | Y |   |   | E | S | E |   | A |
| E |   | B |   |   | I |   |   | T |   | ⁹R | O | C | K |
| R |   | I |   |   | N |   | ¹⁰W | O | O | D |   | K |
|   |   | E |   |   | G |   | H |   |   | R |   | W |
|   |   |   |   |   |   | A | ¹¹B | L | O | O | D |
| ¹²F |   | ¹³C | I | ¹⁴R | C | L | E |   | E |   |   | O |
| I |   | A |   | O |   | E |   |   | A |   |   | D |
| ¹⁵S | O | A | K | S |   | ¹⁶C |   | ¹⁷C |   |   |   |
| H |   | E |   | ¹⁸E | A | G | L | E |   | ¹⁹W | O | L | F |
|   |   |   |   | Y |   | U |   | L |   |   |   |
|   |   |   |   |   | ²⁰B | E | A | V | E | R |   |

Across
1. the location of the island
7. frequently performed as an expression of discovery
8. Cole's parole officer
9. becomes both ancestor and anger
10. "If you discover what's inside the _____, you'll discover what's inside of you."
11. It all looks the same to Cole.
13. the last item carved on Cole's totem
15. the morning ritual to clear Cole's mind
18. the animal associated with staying proud and viewing life differently from a distance
19. the animal associated with the lesson "you need the help of others"
20. the animal associated with lessons of persistence, patience, and ingenuity

Down
1. This state of being scares Cole more than anything else.
2. This rock is carried up the hill and rolled down.
3. the person in charge of Circle Justice meetings
4. It is a memory never forgotten.
5. Cole describes his mom as a scared _____.
6. the lawyer hired by Cole's father
7. Cole is not afraid of this.
10. the animal that is graceful, powerful, and gentle
11. Peter ruins and then fixes Cole's carving of this.
12. Cole takes and eats bits of this from the gulls.
13. Cole's wild laughter mocks the ingredients of his life's _____.
14. nursed Cole right after his rescue
16. tiny, infecting thistles: Devil's _____
17. blames others for his life choices

# Touching Spirit Bear Crossword 2

**Across**
1. It is a memory never forgotten.
4. While recovering, Cole whispers, "My _____!"
5. the animal associated with staying proud and viewing life differently from a distance
7. This state of being scares Cole more than anything else.
9. the victim of Cole's anger
10. They are often not noticed and see things others don't.
11. Cole sleeps there during Peter's visit at first.
12. Cole does this at Edwin and the Spirit Bear.
13. Cole describes his mom as a scared _____.
15. Garvey's nickname for Cole
17. the location of the island
18. Cole takes and eats bits of this from the gulls.
19. blames others for his life choices

**Down**
1. a colorful, comforting blanket
2. To Cole, this is the adult term for passing the buck.
3. the animal associated with lessons of persistence, patience, and ingenuity
4. symbolizes respect
6. Cole's parole officer
7. This rock is carried up the hill and rolled down.
8. the Tlingit Elder
12. the morning ritual to clear Cole's mind
13. It all looks the same to Cole.
14. Peter ruins and then fixes Cole's carving of this.
15. Cole's wild laughter mocks the ingredients of his life's _____.
16. There is no place for this on the island.

Touching Spirit Bear Crossword 2 Answer Key

|   |   |   |   | ¹A | N | G | ²E | R |   |   | ³B |   |
|---|---|---|---|---|---|---|---|---|---|---|---|---|
|   | ⁴F | A | U | L | T |   | ⁵E | A | ⁶G | L | E |   |
|   | E |   |   | . |   |   | F |   | A |   | A |   |
|   | A |   | ⁷A | L | O | ⁸N | E |   | R |   | V |   |
|   | T |   | N |   | O | D |   | R |   | V | E |   |
|   | H |   | C |   | W | W |   | R |   | E | R |   |
| ⁹P | E | T | E | R |   | ¹⁰M | I | C | E |   | Y |   |
|   | R |   | S |   |   |   | N |   | D |   |   |   |
|   |   |   | ¹¹T | E | N | T |   |   | ¹²S | P | I | T |
|   |   |   | O |   |   |   |   |   | O |   |   |   |
|   |   | ¹³B | A | R | ¹⁴B | I | E |   | ¹⁵C | H | A | M | P | ¹⁶ |   |
|   |   | L |   |   | E |   |   |   | A |   | K |   | R |   |
|   |   | O |   | ¹⁷A | L | A | S | K | A |   | ¹⁸F | I | S | H |
|   |   | O |   |   | R |   |   |   | E |   |   | D |   |
|   |   | D |   |   |   |   |   | ¹⁹C | O | L | E |   |   |

**Across**
1. It is a memory never forgotten.
4. While recovering, Cole whispers, "My _____!"
5. the animal associated with staying proud and viewing life differently from a distance
7. This state of being scares Cole more than anything else.
9. the victim of Cole's anger
10. They are often not noticed and see things others don't.
11. Cole sleeps there during Peter's visit at first.
12. Cole does this at Edwin and the Spirit Bear.
13. Cole describes his mom as a scared _____.
15. Garvey's nickname for Cole
17. the location of the island
18. Cole takes and eats bits of this from the gulls.
19. blames others for his life choices

**Down**
1. a colorful, comforting blanket
2. To Cole, this is the adult term for passing the buck.
3. the animal associated with lessons of persistence, patience, and ingenuity
4. symbolizes respect
6. Cole's parole officer
7. This rock is carried up the hill and rolled down.
8. the Tlingit Elder
12. the morning ritual to clear Cole's mind
13. It all looks the same to Cole.
14. Peter ruins and then fixes Cole's carving of this.
15. Cole's wild laughter mocks the ingredients of his life's _____.
16. There is no place for this on the island.

Touching Spirit Bear Crossword 3

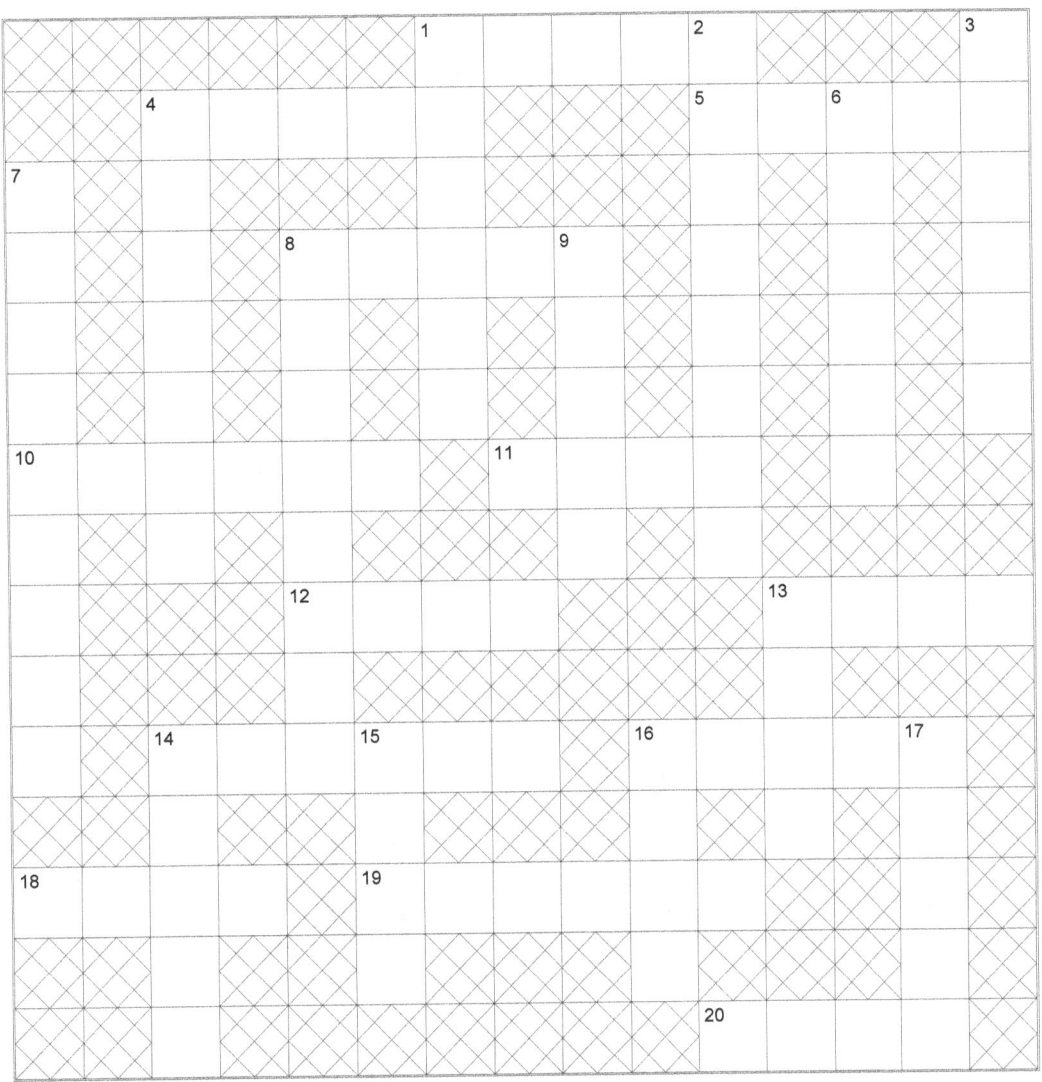

Across
1. It is a memory never forgotten.
4. While recovering, Cole whispers, "My _____!"
5. the animal associated with staying proud and viewing life differently from a distance
8. This state of being scares Cole more than anything else.
10. the person in charge of Circle Justice meetings
11. They are often not noticed and see things others don't.
12. Cole sleeps there during Peter's visit at first.
13. Cole does this at Edwin and the Spirit Bear.
14. Cole describes his mom as a scared _____.
16. Garvey's nickname for Cole
18. "If you discover what's inside the _____, you'll discover what's inside of you."
19. the location of the island
20. Cole saves a handful of this but later discards it.

Down
1. a colorful, comforting blanket
2. To Cole, this is the adult term for passing the buck.
3. the animal associated with lessons of persistence, patience, and ingenuity
4. symbolizes respect
6. Cole's parole officer
7. the lawyer hired by Cole's father
8. This rock is carried up the hill and rolled down.
9. the Tlingit Elder
13. the morning ritual to clear Cole's mind
14. It all looks the same to Cole.
15. Peter ruins and then fixes Cole's carving of this.
16. Cole's wild laughter mocks the ingredients of his life's _____.
17. the victim of Cole's anger

Touching Spirit Bear Crossword 3 Answer Key

**Across**
1. It is a memory never forgotten.
4. While recovering, Cole whispers, "My _____!"
5. the animal associated with staying proud and viewing life differently from a distance
8. This state of being scares Cole more than anything else.
10. the person in charge of Circle Justice meetings
11. They are often not noticed and see things others don't.
12. Cole sleeps there during Peter's visit at first.
13. Cole does this at Edwin and the Spirit Bear.
14. Cole describes his mom as a scared _____.
16. Garvey's nickname for Cole
18. "If you discover what's inside the _____, you'll discover what's inside of you."
19. the location of the island
20. Cole saves a handful of this but later discards it.

**Down**
1. a colorful, comforting blanket
2. To Cole, this is the adult term for passing the buck.
3. the animal associated with lessons of persistence, patience, and ingenuity
4. symbolizes respect
6. Cole's parole officer
7. the lawyer hired by Cole's father
8. This rock is carried up the hill and rolled down.
9. the Tlingit Elder
13. the morning ritual to clear Cole's mind
14. It all looks the same to Cole.
15. Peter ruins and then fixes Cole's carving of this.
16. Cole's wild laughter mocks the ingredients of his life's _____.
17. the victim of Cole's anger

# Touching Spirit Bear Crossword 4

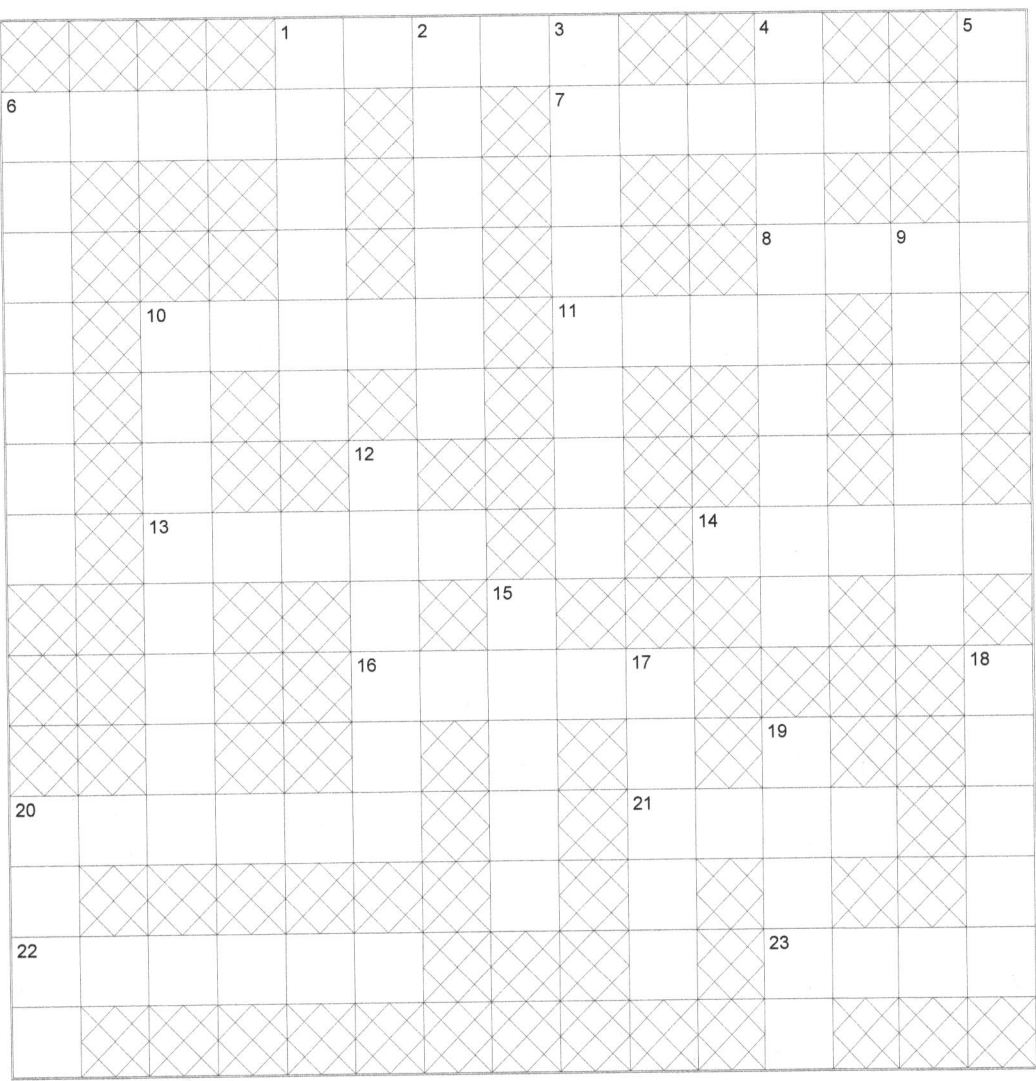

**Across**
1. It is a memory never forgotten.
6. While recovering, Cole whispers, "My _____!"
7. the animal associated with staying proud and viewing life differently from a distance
8. Cole's wild laughter mocks the ingredients of his life's _____.
10. This state of being scares Cole more than anything else.
11. becomes both ancestor and anger
13. the Tlingit Elder
14. nursed Cole right after his rescue
16. Garvey's nickname for Cole
20. Cole describes his mom as a scared _____.
21. Cole sleeps there during Peter's visit at first.
22. the location of the island
23. Cole takes and eats bits of this from the gulls.

**Down**
1. a colorful, comforting blanket
2. Cole's parole officer
3. To Cole, this is the adult term for passing the buck.
4. the lawyer hired by Cole's father
5. blames others for his life choices
6. symbolizes respect
9. the person in charge of Circle Justice meetings
10. This rock is carried up the hill and rolled down.
12. the last item carved on Cole's totem
15. frequently performed as an expression of discovery
17. the victim of Cole's anger
18. The gulls pick at Cole's
19. an instrument of destruction or healing
20. Peter ruins and then fixes Cole's carving of this.

# Touching Spirit Bear Crossword 4 Answer Key

|   |   |   |   | 1 A | 2 N | 3 G | E | R |   | 4 B |   | 5 C |
|---|---|---|---|---|---|---|---|---|---|---|---|---|
| 6 F | A | U | L | T |   | A |   | 7 E | A | G | L | O |
| E |   |   |   | . |   | R |   | F |   | A |   | L |
| A |   |   |   | O |   | V |   | E |   | 8 C | 9 A | K E |
| T |   | 10 A | L | O | N | E |   | 11 R | O | C | K |   |
| H |   | N |   | W |   | Y |   | R |   | W |   | E |
| E |   | C |   |   | 12 C |   |   | E |   | O |   | P |
| R |   | 13 E | D | W | I | N |   | D |   | 14 R | O | S E Y |
|   |   | S |   |   | R |   | 15 D |   |   | D |   | R |
|   |   | T |   | 16 C | H | A | M | 17 P |   |   |   | 18 F |
|   |   | O |   | L |   |   | N | E |   | 19 K |   | L |
| 20 B | A | R | B | I | E |   | C | T |   | N | T | E |
| E |   |   |   | E |   |   | E | E |   | I |   | S |
| 22 A | L | A | S | K | A |   |   | R |   | 23 F | I | S H |
| R |   |   |   |   |   |   |   | E |   |   |   |   |

## Across
1. It is a memory never forgotten.
6. While recovering, Cole whispers, "My _____!"
7. the animal associated with staying proud and viewing life differently from a distance
8. Cole's wild laughter mocks the ingredients of his life's _____.
10. This state of being scares Cole more than anything else.
11. becomes both ancestor and anger
13. the Tlingit Elder
14. nursed Cole right after his rescue
16. Garvey's nickname for Cole
20. Cole describes his mom as a scared _____.
21. Cole sleeps there during Peter's visit at first.
22. the location of the island
23. Cole takes and eats bits of this from the gulls.

## Down
1. a colorful, comforting blanket
2. Cole's parole officer
3. To Cole, this is the adult term for passing the buck.
4. the lawyer hired by Cole's father
5. blames others for his life choices
6. symbolizes respect
9. the person in charge of Circle Justice meetings
10. This rock is carried up the hill and rolled down.
12. the last item carved on Cole's totem
15. frequently performed as an expression of discovery
17. the victim of Cole's anger
18. The gulls pick at Cole's
19. an instrument of destruction or healing
20. Peter ruins and then fixes Cole's carving of this.

Touching Spirit Bear

| CLUB | KNIFE | SPIT | BEAVER | FEATHER |
|---|---|---|---|---|
| TENT | ALASKA | SUPPER | AT.ÓOW | ALONE |
| TOTEM | ANGER | FREE SPACE | SOAK | REFERRED |
| YOURSELF | BIRTHDAY | CIRCLE | KEEPER | BLOOD |
| BLACKWOOD | JUSTICE | CAKE | PRIDE | COLE |

Touching Spirit Bear

| CHAMP | EAGLE | DANCE | INVISIBLE | TRUST |
|---|---|---|---|---|
| ROSEY | BARBIE | GARVEY | SUICIDE | WOLF |
| HAIR | WILLIAM | FREE SPACE | SHELTER | HOTDOG |
| MIKAELSEN | SPARROWS | WOOD | BEAR | FAULT |
| ROCK | DYING | MICE | FLESH | SPIRIT |

## Touching Spirit Bear

| CHAMP | BIRTHDAY | COLE | YOURSELF | FEATHER |
|---|---|---|---|---|
| TOTEM | SUICIDE | BARBIE | BLACKWOOD | TRUST |
| CLUB | KEEPER | FREE SPACE | WOOD | ANCESTOR |
| FORGIVES | DYING | SOAK | ROSEY | EDWIN |
| SHELTER | SPARROWS | BEAR | SUPPER | FAULT |

## Touching Spirit Bear

| PETER | HOTDOG | ROCK | EAGLE | ANGER |
|---|---|---|---|---|
| BLOOD | PRIDE | FLESH | MOUSE | KNIFE |
| SPIRIT | AT.ÓOW | FREE SPACE | SPIT | INVISIBLE |
| BEAVER | WILLIAM | TLINGIT | SWIM | WOLF |
| MINNEAPOLIS | MICE | MIKAELSEN | TENT | DANCE |

Copyrighted

## Touching Spirit Bear

| MICE | MOUSE | EAGLE | SWIM | SOAK |
|---|---|---|---|---|
| COLE | TRUST | DANCE | CAKE | KNIFE |
| BARBIE | DYING | FREE SPACE | REFERRED | ROSEY |
| CHAMP | BEAVER | WOOD | TLINGIT | BIRTHDAY |
| BLACKWOOD | BLOOD | INVISIBLE | AT.ÓOW | ROCK |

## Touching Spirit Bear

| ALASKA | SPARROWS | EDWIN | WILLIAM | TENT |
|---|---|---|---|---|
| SUICIDE | ANCESTOR | YOURSELF | FORGIVES | BEAR |
| PETER | SPIRIT | FREE SPACE | KEEPER | WOLF |
| PRIDE | TOTEM | SPIT | HAIR | WHALE |
| GARVEY | CLUB | MIKAELSEN | ALONE | SHELTER |

Touching Spirit Bear

| WOLF | SUPPER | BIRTHDAY | SPIT | SOAK |
|---|---|---|---|---|
| BLOOD | DYING | MIKAELSEN | SUICIDE | BLACKWOOD |
| FISH | HOTDOG | FREE SPACE | SHELTER | BEAR |
| TENT | ROCK | CIRCLE | ALONE | EDWIN |
| WOOD | ANCESTOR | KNIFE | ROSEY | EAGLE |

Touching Spirit Bear

| FEATHER | BARBIE | MICE | BEAVER | FLESH |
|---|---|---|---|---|
| PETER | REFERRED | CAKE | FAULT | TLINGIT |
| COLE | MOUSE | FREE SPACE | JUSTICE | YOURSELF |
| AT.ÓOW | DANCE | SWIM | TRUST | MINNEAPOLIS |
| PRIDE | GARVEY | SPIRIT | WHALE | HAIR |

## Touching Spirit Bear

| YOURSELF | KEEPER | SWIM | ANGER | CHAMP |
| --- | --- | --- | --- | --- |
| CIRCLE | MINNEAPOLIS | ALONE | FISH | WHALE |
| BEAVER | TOTEM | FREE SPACE | PETER | TLINGIT |
| HOTDOG | GARVEY | SPIRIT | MIKAELSEN | INVISIBLE |
| CAKE | DANCE | JUSTICE | ANCESTOR | FAULT |

## Touching Spirit Bear

| DYING | TRUST | HAIR | SOAK | SPIT |
| --- | --- | --- | --- | --- |
| MOUSE | FLESH | ROSEY | FEATHER | REFERRED |
| EDWIN | EAGLE | FREE SPACE | KNIFE | PRIDE |
| ROCK | WOLF | MICE | WOOD | BLOOD |
| SPARROWS | BEAR | SUPPER | FORGIVES | AT.ÓOW |

Touching Spirit Bear

| EAGLE | CIRCLE | TENT | SWIM | FORGIVES |
|---|---|---|---|---|
| BIRTHDAY | SPARROWS | SHELTER | REFERRED | SPIT |
| BEAR | SOAK | FREE SPACE | TOTEM | DYING |
| DANCE | TRUST | JUSTICE | WOLF | FAULT |
| SUICIDE | SUPPER | PETER | ALASKA | MIKAELSEN |

Touching Spirit Bear

| INVISIBLE | SPIRIT | FLESH | HOTDOG | MICE |
|---|---|---|---|---|
| EDWIN | COLE | ANGER | BARBIE | WILLIAM |
| TLINGIT | AT.ÓOW | FREE SPACE | PRIDE | BLACKWOOD |
| MOUSE | CAKE | FEATHER | KNIFE | YOURSELF |
| ROSEY | CLUB | ALONE | WHALE | HAIR |

## Touching Spirit Bear

| BARBIE | BLOOD | WILLIAM | BEAR | WOOD |
|--------|-------|---------|------|------|
| HOTDOG | SUPPER | FAULT | REFERRED | BIRTHDAY |
| ALASKA | TLINGIT | FREE SPACE | SPIRIT | BEAVER |
| EAGLE | YOURSELF | AT.OOW | BLACKWOOD | DYING |
| WHALE | SPIT | CHAMP | ROCK | FLESH |

## Touching Spirit Bear

| ANGER | HAIR | ALONE | SHELTER | KEEPER |
|-------|------|-------|---------|--------|
| FISH | COLE | FORGIVES | TRUST | SWIM |
| CLUB | CIRCLE | FREE SPACE | JUSTICE | INVISIBLE |
| KNIFE | SPARROWS | PETER | EDWIN | FEATHER |
| CAKE | DANCE | ROSEY | TOTEM | SUICIDE |

## Touching Spirit Bear

| GARVEY | PRIDE | WOOD | TOTEM | ALASKA |
|---|---|---|---|---|
| PETER | DYING | INVISIBLE | ANCESTOR | SPARROWS |
| MINNEAPOLIS | ROSEY | FREE SPACE | TRUST | KEEPER |
| SUPPER | FAULT | BLOOD | CHAMP | YOURSELF |
| JUSTICE | HAIR | EAGLE | ALONE | TENT |

## Touching Spirit Bear

| EDWIN | DANCE | BEAR | BLACKWOOD | SOAK |
|---|---|---|---|---|
| WOLF | SHELTER | FISH | CLUB | TLINGIT |
| COLE | SWIM | FREE SPACE | CIRCLE | SUICIDE |
| ANGER | MOUSE | FLESH | REFERRED | FEATHER |
| WILLIAM | WHALE | AT.ÓOW | BARBIE | CAKE |

Touching Spirit Bear

| SHELTER | BLACKWOOD | TENT | MOUSE | BARBIE |
|---------|-----------|------|-------|--------|
| FLESH | FORGIVES | SPIRIT | CLUB | JUSTICE |
| GARVEY | KEEPER | FREE SPACE | HOTDOG | PRIDE |
| YOURSELF | TLINGIT | MIKAELSEN | FEATHER | CIRCLE |
| ROSEY | BLOOD | ANCESTOR | PETER | MICE |

Touching Spirit Bear

| FAULT | SPARROWS | AT.ÓOW | EDWIN | BIRTHDAY |
|-------|----------|--------|-------|----------|
| INVISIBLE | SWIM | SUICIDE | HAIR | BEAR |
| ANGER | WOLF | FREE SPACE | DYING | DANCE |
| WHALE | CHAMP | WOOD | TRUST | WILLIAM |
| FISH | ALASKA | COLE | MINNEAPOLIS | SPIT |

## Touching Spirit Bear

| TOTEM | SWIM | INVISIBLE | CLUB | FLESH |
|---|---|---|---|---|
| BEAR | ANGER | WILLIAM | KNIFE | PETER |
| ROSEY | SPIRIT | FREE SPACE | ROCK | REFERRED |
| EDWIN | DANCE | SPARROWS | TENT | BLACKWOOD |
| YOURSELF | DYING | MIKAELSEN | SUPPER | TRUST |

## Touching Spirit Bear

| SUICIDE | ANCESTOR | BLOOD | HOTDOG | MICE |
|---|---|---|---|---|
| FAULT | CAKE | FEATHER | CHAMP | WOOD |
| KEEPER | TLINGIT | FREE SPACE | EAGLE | FISH |
| BEAVER | MINNEAPOLIS | COLE | PRIDE | MOUSE |
| WOLF | HAIR | SHELTER | CIRCLE | BARBIE |

## Touching Spirit Bear

| FLESH | KEEPER | WHALE | SWIM | PETER |
|---|---|---|---|---|
| MIKAELSEN | EAGLE | BLACKWOOD | SHELTER | AT.OOW |
| FORGIVES | WOOD | FREE SPACE | TLINGIT | BLOOD |
| SPIT | HOTDOG | CAKE | SOAK | BARBIE |
| SUPPER | DANCE | WILLIAM | ANGER | REFERRED |

## Touching Spirit Bear

| ROSEY | JUSTICE | TOTEM | SPIRIT | INVISIBLE |
|---|---|---|---|---|
| ANCESTOR | TRUST | BEAVER | CIRCLE | ALONE |
| CHAMP | ROCK | FREE SPACE | KNIFE | PRIDE |
| HAIR | TENT | FISH | COLE | BIRTHDAY |
| EDWIN | SUICIDE | GARVEY | MINNEAPOLIS | FEATHER |

## Touching Spirit Bear

| SUPPER | BLOOD | ANCESTOR | CHAMP | WOOD |
|---|---|---|---|---|
| PRIDE | WOLF | TOTEM | BEAVER | JUSTICE |
| MINNEAPOLIS | WILLIAM | FREE SPACE | TRUST | SPARROWS |
| SPIT | MICE | DYING | WHALE | MIKAELSEN |
| ROSEY | EAGLE | REFERRED | COLE | FAULT |

## Touching Spirit Bear

| KEEPER | MOUSE | EDWIN | BLACKWOOD | DANCE |
|---|---|---|---|---|
| SWIM | AT.ÓOW | CIRCLE | SHELTER | ALASKA |
| ROCK | YOURSELF | FREE SPACE | SOAK | FEATHER |
| HOTDOG | SPIRIT | ALONE | HAIR | FORGIVES |
| SUICIDE | ANGER | CLUB | BARBIE | BIRTHDAY |

## Touching Spirit Bear

| ROCK | AT.ÓOW | HOTDOG | KNIFE | REFERRED |
|---|---|---|---|---|
| SPIT | CIRCLE | BEAVER | COLE | KEEPER |
| MIKAELSEN | FEATHER | FREE SPACE | DYING | PRIDE |
| SWIM | CHAMP | SPARROWS | BLACKWOOD | FISH |
| WOLF | FLESH | HAIR | INVISIBLE | MOUSE |

## Touching Spirit Bear

| TOTEM | SOAK | ANGER | MICE | BEAR |
|---|---|---|---|---|
| CLUB | DANCE | TRUST | TENT | WILLIAM |
| WHALE | FAULT | FREE SPACE | MINNEAPOLIS | ALONE |
| SPIRIT | YOURSELF | SUPPER | SUICIDE | CAKE |
| PETER | TLINGIT | EDWIN | JUSTICE | EAGLE |

## Touching Spirit Bear

| | | | | |
|---|---|---|---|---|
| ANCESTOR | ROCK | FISH | HAIR | BARBIE |
| ANGER | FAULT | INVISIBLE | FLESH | COLE |
| EDWIN | JUSTICE | FREE SPACE | BIRTHDAY | WILLIAM |
| MOUSE | TOTEM | SOAK | KNIFE | MINNEAPOLIS |
| FEATHER | SPARROWS | ALONE | SPIT | TENT |

## Touching Spirit Bear

| | | | | |
|---|---|---|---|---|
| EAGLE | DANCE | TLINGIT | REFERRED | AT.ÓOW |
| CAKE | CHAMP | SUPPER | HOTDOG | TRUST |
| SWIM | PRIDE | FREE SPACE | MIKAELSEN | DYING |
| PETER | BEAVER | CLUB | CIRCLE | BLOOD |
| YOURSELF | WOOD | BLACKWOOD | BEAR | ALASKA |

## Touching Spirit Bear

| BARBIE | HOTDOG | MIKAELSEN | FLESH | BEAVER |
|---|---|---|---|---|
| FORGIVES | SHELTER | ANGER | TRUST | AT.ÓOW |
| WILLIAM | EDWIN | FREE SPACE | BLOOD | SPIT |
| ROSEY | CLUB | MINNEAPOLIS | WOOD | INVISIBLE |
| SPARROWS | BIRTHDAY | SPIRIT | DANCE | MICE |

## Touching Spirit Bear

| HAIR | FAULT | CHAMP | PETER | COLE |
|---|---|---|---|---|
| ROCK | ANCESTOR | TOTEM | DYING | CAKE |
| YOURSELF | PRIDE | FREE SPACE | GARVEY | TLINGIT |
| SWIM | WOLF | TENT | WHALE | REFERRED |
| EAGLE | FEATHER | BLACKWOOD | MOUSE | KEEPER |

## Touching Spirit Bear

| | | | | |
|---|---|---|---|---|
| TRUST | SUICIDE | SPIRIT | TOTEM | WHALE |
| ALASKA | WOLF | ALONE | SWIM | BIRTHDAY |
| KEEPER | SPIT | FREE SPACE | FORGIVES | JUSTICE |
| MOUSE | ROSEY | REFERRED | YOURSELF | CAKE |
| MICE | CHAMP | DYING | BEAR | WILLIAM |

## Touching Spirit Bear

| | | | | |
|---|---|---|---|---|
| COLE | BLACKWOOD | FISH | MINNEAPOLIS | SHELTER |
| ROCK | BLOOD | BEAVER | SUPPER | ANGER |
| HAIR | PRIDE | FREE SPACE | FEATHER | MIKAELSEN |
| CLUB | TENT | GARVEY | FLESH | HOTDOG |
| KNIFE | EDWIN | ANCESTOR | CIRCLE | EAGLE |

Touching Spirit Bear Vocabulary Word List

1. ACKNOWLEDGED — showed a sign of awareness or acceptance
2. ALTERNATIVE — a choice or another option
3. ANCESTORS — family members who have lived before one's own time
4. AWKWARD — inconvenient; difficult; uncomfortable; clumsy
5. BANISHMENT — removal from society; exile
6. BIZARRE — strange; weird
7. BRANDISHED — waved
8. CEASED — stopped
9. COAXING — gentle attempts to persuade or influence
10. COMPOSURE — calmness
11. CONJURING — bringing to mind; recalling
12. CONSCIOUS — known to oneself; aware
13. CONSEQUENCES — effects or results
14. DAWDLED — wasted time; moved very slowly
15. DEFIANTLY — willfully or disobediently
16. DEFIED — challenged; boldly resisted or went against
17. DELIBERATELY — slowly; carefully; thoughtfully
18. EMERGED — came out
19. ENDURE — to bear or put up with
20. FEIGNED — pretended
21. FESTER — to become an irritating, infected, sore spot
22. FREQUENT — often
23. FRIGID — very cold; freezing
24. GLUTTONOUS — greedy
25. GORGED — stuffed with food

| # | Word | Definition |
|---|---|---|
| 26. | GRIMACING | making a facial expression that indicates disapproval, pain, or difficulty |
| 27. | GRUB | food |
| 28. | HAGGARD | tired-looking; an unhealthy appearance |
| 29. | HALLUCINATION | a vision; figment of the imagination |
| 30. | HYPNOTIC | fascinating; having a sleep-inducing effect |
| 31. | IMPATIENT | unable to wait; not accepting delay |
| 32. | INCESSANT | constant |
| 33. | INEVITABLE | can't be avoided; bound to happen |
| 34. | INFERNO | a very intense fire |
| 35. | INGENUITY | cleverness |
| 36. | INSIGNIFICANT | not important; meaningless |
| 37. | INSTINCT | natural inborn ability |
| 38. | INVISIBLE | not able to be seen or noticed |
| 39. | IRKED | irritated; annoyed; bothered |
| 40. | IRRITATION | annoyance |
| 41. | MANEUVERED | steered or managed with skill |
| 42. | MANIPULATED | controlled |
| 43. | MAULED | injured by a savage animal attack |
| 44. | MENACINGLY | in a threatening manner |
| 45. | MESMERIZE | to put into a trance; bewitch |
| 46. | MIGRATE | to move or travel from one place to another |
| 47. | MOCKED | made fun of |
| 48. | MONOTONOUS | boring; lacking in variety |
| 49. | OMEN | a sign or warning |
| 50. | ORBS | round objects |
| 51. | PERSISTENT | not giving up; continuing in spite of obstacles |
| 52. | POTENTIAL | the ability or capability |

| | | |
|---|---|---|
| 53. | PURSUIT | the act of chasing or going after something |
| 54. | QUIVERED | trembled; vibrated |
| 55. | REDEMPTION | forgiveness through making up for a wrongdoing |
| 56. | REGRET | a feeling of sorrow or remorse |
| 57. | REHABILITATION | the act of returning to good condition or normalcy |
| 58. | RELINQUISH | to release or surrender |
| 59. | RELUCTANTLY | unwillingly; with hesitation |
| 60. | REVERENTLY | respectfully |
| 61. | SARCASM | the use of words to express bitterness or mockery; scorn |
| 62. | SAVORING | slowly and thoroughly enjoying something |
| 63. | SCAVENGER | one who gathers things thrown away by others |
| 64. | SHROUDED | hidden or covered |
| 65. | SOLITARY | alone; singular |
| 66. | SPASMED | twitched or seized |
| 67. | STARK | bleak; bare; very plain |
| 68. | STIFLED | withheld; suppressed; ended by force |
| 69. | STUPOROUS | dazed |
| 70. | SUBMISSION | the act of giving in to a stronger power |
| 71. | TAUNTED | teased; blamed or scolded in an insulting way |
| 72. | TENTATIVE | very careful; with hesitation; unsure |
| 73. | TRANCE | the state of being semi-aware; in a daze |
| 74. | TRAUMA | painful damage |
| 75. | TRAWLER | a type of fishing boat |
| 76. | TREACHEROUS | dangerous; hazardous |
| 77. | UTTER | total; complete |
| 78. | VENGEANCE | revenge; punishment |
| 79. | VIOLATED | broke a law, rule, agreement, or promise |

| | | |
|---|---|---|
| 80. VOWED | | promised; pledged |
| 81. VULNERABLE | | defenseless and exposed |
| 82. WARILY | | cautiously |
| 83. WEARILY | | in a tired manner |
| 84. WINCING | | drawing back or tensing the body or face |

Touching Spirit Bear Vocabulary Fill in the Blank 1

_____ 1. withheld; suppressed; ended by force

_____ 2. annoyance

_____ 3. wasted time; moved very slowly

_____ 4. the act of giving in to a stronger power

_____ 5. respectfully

_____ 6. the act of returning to good condition or normalcy

_____ 7. willfully or disobediently

_____ 8. controlled

_____ 9. a choice or another option

_____ 10. a vision; figment of the imagination

_____ 11. in a tired manner

_____ 12. to become an irritating, infected, sore spot

_____ 13. known to oneself; aware

_____ 14. waved

_____ 15. made fun of

_____ 16. tired-looking; an unhealthy appearance

_____ 17. a sign or warning

_____ 18. in a threatening manner

_____ 19. to move or travel from one place to another

_____ 20. broke a law, rule, agreement, or promise

Touching Spirit Bear Vocabulary Fill in the Blank 1 Answer Key

| Word | Definition |
|---|---|
| STIFLED | 1. withheld; suppressed; ended by force |
| IRRITATION | 2. annoyance |
| DAWDLED | 3. wasted time; moved very slowly |
| SUBMISSION | 4. the act of giving in to a stronger power |
| REVERENTLY | 5. respectfully |
| REHABILITATION | 6. the act of returning to good condition or normalcy |
| DEFIANTLY | 7. willfully or disobediently |
| MANIPULATED | 8. controlled |
| ALTERNATIVE | 9. a choice or another option |
| HALLUCINATION | 10. a vision; figment of the imagination |
| WEARILY | 11. in a tired manner |
| FESTER | 12. to become an irritating, infected, sore spot |
| CONSCIOUS | 13. known to oneself; aware |
| BRANDISHED | 14. waved |
| MOCKED | 15. made fun of |
| HAGGARD | 16. tired-looking; an unhealthy appearance |
| OMEN | 17. a sign or warning |
| MENACINGLY | 18. in a threatening manner |
| MIGRATE | 19. to move or travel from one place to another |
| VIOLATED | 20. broke a law, rule, agreement, or promise |

Touching Spirit Bear Vocabulary Fill in the Blank 2

_____ 1. bringing to mind; recalling

_____ 2. annoyance

_____ 3. round objects

_____ 4. to bear or put up with

_____ 5. in a threatening manner

_____ 6. can't be avoided; bound to happen

_____ 7. inconvenient; difficult; uncomfortable; clumsy

_____ 8. natural inborn ability

_____ 9. to release or surrender

_____ 10. slowly and thoroughly enjoying something

_____ 11. boring; lacking in variety

_____ 12. unable to wait; not accepting delay

_____ 13. twitched or seized

_____ 14. to move or travel from one place to another

_____ 15. revenge; punishment

_____ 16. a type of fishing boat

_____ 17. fascinating; having a sleep-inducing effect

_____ 18. strange; weird

_____ 19. trembled; vibrated

_____ 20. removal from society; exile

Touching Spirit Bear Vocabulary Fill in the Blank 2 Answer Key

| Word | Definition |
|---|---|
| CONJURING | 1. bringing to mind; recalling |
| IRRITATION | 2. annoyance |
| ORBS | 3. round objects |
| ENDURE | 4. to bear or put up with |
| MENACINGLY | 5. in a threatening manner |
| INEVITABLE | 6. can't be avoided; bound to happen |
| AWKWARD | 7. inconvenient; difficult; uncomfortable; clumsy |
| INSTINCT | 8. natural inborn ability |
| RELINQUISH | 9. to release or surrender |
| SAVORING | 10. slowly and thoroughly enjoying something |
| MONOTONOUS | 11. boring; lacking in variety |
| IMPATIENT | 12. unable to wait; not accepting delay |
| SPASMED | 13. twitched or seized |
| MIGRATE | 14. to move or travel from one place to another |
| VENGEANCE | 15. revenge; punishment |
| TRAWLER | 16. a type of fishing boat |
| HYPNOTIC | 17. fascinating; having a sleep-inducing effect |
| BIZARRE | 18. strange; weird |
| QUIVERED | 19. trembled; vibrated |
| BANISHMENT | 20. removal from society; exile |

Touching Spirit Bear Vocabulary Fill in the Blank 3

_____  1. a feeling of sorrow or remorse

_____  2. not important; meaningless

_____  3. wasted time; moved very slowly

_____  4. not able to be seen or noticed

_____  5. showed a sign of awareness or acceptance

_____  6. unwillingly; with hesitation

_____  7. round objects

_____  8. the ability or capability

_____  9. teased; blamed or scolded in an insulting way

_____  10. the use of words to express bitterness or mockery; scorn

_____  11. very careful; with hesitation; unsure

_____  12. drawing back or tensing the body or face

_____  13. not giving up; continuing in spite of obstacles

_____  14. promised; pledged

_____  15. defenseless and exposed

_____  16. the act of chasing or going after something

_____  17. effects or results

_____  18. greedy

_____  19. family members who have lived before one's own time

_____  20. cleverness

Touching Spirit Bear Vocabulary Fill in the Blank 3 Answer Key

| Word | Definition |
|---|---|
| REGRET | 1. a feeling of sorrow or remorse |
| INSIGNIFICANT | 2. not important; meaningless |
| DAWDLED | 3. wasted time; moved very slowly |
| INVISIBLE | 4. not able to be seen or noticed |
| ACKNOWLEDGED | 5. showed a sign of awareness or acceptance |
| RELUCTANTLY | 6. unwillingly; with hesitation |
| ORBS | 7. round objects |
| POTENTIAL | 8. the ability or capability |
| TAUNTED | 9. teased; blamed or scolded in an insulting way |
| SARCASM | 10. the use of words to express bitterness or mockery; scorn |
| TENTATIVE | 11. very careful; with hesitation; unsure |
| WINCING | 12. drawing back or tensing the body or face |
| PERSISTENT | 13. not giving up; continuing in spite of obstacles |
| VOWED | 14. promised; pledged |
| VULNERABLE | 15. defenseless and exposed |
| PURSUIT | 16. the act of chasing or going after something |
| CONSEQUENCES | 17. effects or results |
| GLUTTONOUS | 18. greedy |
| ANCESTORS | 19. family members who have lived before one's own time |
| INGENUITY | 20. cleverness |

Touching Spirit Bear Vocabulary Fill in the Blank 4

_____  1. can't be avoided; bound to happen

_____  2. inconvenient; difficult; uncomfortable; clumsy

_____  3. painful damage

_____  4. greedy

_____  5. bringing to mind; recalling

_____  6. unable to wait; not accepting delay

_____  7. calmness

_____  8. alone; singular

_____  9. not giving up; continuing in spite of obstacles

_____  10. not able to be seen or noticed

_____  11. total; complete

_____  12. the act of giving in to a stronger power

_____  13. stopped

_____  14. often

_____  15. steered or managed with skill

_____  16. a feeling of sorrow or remorse

_____  17. known to oneself; aware

_____  18. injured by a savage animal attack

_____  19. fascinating; having a sleep-inducing effect

_____  20. the state of being semi-aware; in a daze

Touching Spirit Bear Vocabulary Fill in the Blank 4 Answer Key

| | |
|---|---|
| INEVITABLE | 1. can't be avoided; bound to happen |
| AWKWARD | 2. inconvenient; difficult; uncomfortable; clumsy |
| TRAUMA | 3. painful damage |
| GLUTTONOUS | 4. greedy |
| CONJURING | 5. bringing to mind; recalling |
| IMPATIENT | 6. unable to wait; not accepting delay |
| COMPOSURE | 7. calmness |
| SOLITARY | 8. alone; singular |
| PERSISTENT | 9. not giving up; continuing in spite of obstacles |
| INVISIBLE | 10. not able to be seen or noticed |
| UTTER | 11. total; complete |
| SUBMISSION | 12. the act of giving in to a stronger power |
| CEASED | 13. stopped |
| FREQUENT | 14. often |
| MANEUVERED | 15. steered or managed with skill |
| REGRET | 16. a feeling of sorrow or remorse |
| CONSCIOUS | 17. known to oneself; aware |
| MAULED | 18. injured by a savage animal attack |
| HYPNOTIC | 19. fascinating; having a sleep-inducing effect |
| TRANCE | 20. the state of being semi-aware; in a daze |

Touching Spirit Bear Matching 1

1. INGENUITY — A. making a facial expression that indicates disapproval, pain, or difficulty
2. MANEUVERED — B. the act of returning to good condition or normalcy
3. MOCKED — C. drawing back or tensing the body or face
4. SPASMED — D. revenge; punishment
5. SARCASM — E. a vision; figment of the imagination
6. TRAUMA — F. cleverness
7. REHABILITATION — G. bleak; bare; very plain
8. HALLUCINATION — H. to put into a trance; bewitch
9. RELUCTANTLY — I. teased; blamed or scolded in an insulting way
10. STARK — J. unwillingly; with hesitation
11. SAVORING — K. inconvenient; difficult; uncomfortable; clumsy
12. WEARILY — L. painful damage
13. MESMERIZE — M. in a tired manner
14. REVERENTLY — N. pretended
15. TAUNTED — O. greedy
16. AWKWARD — P. steered or managed with skill
17. FEIGNED — Q. respectfully
18. COAXING — R. made fun of
19. WINCING — S. the use of words to express bitterness or mockery; scorn
20. GLUTTONOUS — T. slowly and thoroughly enjoying something
21. VENGEANCE — U. boring; lacking in variety
22. GRIMACING — V. not giving up; continuing in spite of obstacles
23. CONSEQUENCES — W. gentle attempts to persuade or influence
24. PERSISTENT — X. twitched or seized
25. MONOTONOUS — Y. effects or results

Touching Spirit Bear Matching 1 Answer Key

| | | | |
|---|---|---|---|
| F | 1. INGENUITY | A. | making a facial expression that indicates disapproval, pain, or difficulty |
| P | 2. MANEUVERED | B. | the act of returning to good condition or normalcy |
| R | 3. MOCKED | C. | drawing back or tensing the body or face |
| X | 4. SPASMED | D. | revenge; punishment |
| S | 5. SARCASM | E. | a vision; figment of the imagination |
| L | 6. TRAUMA | F. | cleverness |
| B | 7. REHABILITATION | G. | bleak; bare; very plain |
| E | 8. HALLUCINATION | H. | to put into a trance; bewitch |
| J | 9. RELUCTANTLY | I. | teased; blamed or scolded in an insulting way |
| G | 10. STARK | J. | unwillingly; with hesitation |
| T | 11. SAVORING | K. | inconvenient; difficult; uncomfortable; clumsy |
| M | 12. WEARILY | L. | painful damage |
| H | 13. MESMERIZE | M. | in a tired manner |
| Q | 14. REVERENTLY | N. | pretended |
| I | 15. TAUNTED | O. | greedy |
| K | 16. AWKWARD | P. | steered or managed with skill |
| N | 17. FEIGNED | Q. | respectfully |
| W | 18. COAXING | R. | made fun of |
| C | 19. WINCING | S. | the use of words to express bitterness or mockery; scorn |
| O | 20. GLUTTONOUS | T. | slowly and thoroughly enjoying something |
| D | 21. VENGEANCE | U. | boring; lacking in variety |
| A | 22. GRIMACING | V. | not giving up; continuing in spite of obstacles |
| Y | 23. CONSEQUENCES | W. | gentle attempts to persuade or influence |
| V | 24. PERSISTENT | X. | twitched or seized |
| U | 25. MONOTONOUS | Y. | effects or results |

Touching Spirit Bear Matching 2

1. ALTERNATIVE — A. challenged; boldly resisted or went against
2. PURSUIT — B. cleverness
3. GORGED — C. not able to be seen or noticed
4. DELIBERATELY — D. effects or results
5. VENGEANCE — E. slowly; carefully; thoughtfully
6. TRAWLER — F. can't be avoided; bound to happen
7. IRRITATION — G. greedy
8. INVISIBLE — H. stuffed with food
9. MAULED — I. the act of chasing or going after something
10. INCESSANT — J. slowly and thoroughly enjoying something
11. INEVITABLE — K. constant
12. GLUTTONOUS — L. a choice or another option
13. CEASED — M. injured by a savage animal attack
14. INFERNO — N. revenge; punishment
15. MONOTONOUS — O. willfully or disobediently
16. SAVORING — P. total; complete
17. DEFIED — Q. boring; lacking in variety
18. UTTER — R. to move or travel from one place to another
19. CONSEQUENCES — S. stopped
20. MIGRATE — T. annoyance
21. VULNERABLE — U. a very intense fire
22. INGENUITY — V. defenseless and exposed
23. DEFIANTLY — W. very cold; freezing
24. FRIGID — X. a type of fishing boat
25. PERSISTENT — Y. not giving up; continuing in spite of obstacles

# Touching Spirit Bear Matching 2 Answer Key

| | | | |
|---|---|---|---|
| L | 1. ALTERNATIVE | A. | challenged; boldly resisted or went against |
| I | 2. PURSUIT | B. | cleverness |
| H | 3. GORGED | C. | not able to be seen or noticed |
| E | 4. DELIBERATELY | D. | effects or results |
| N | 5. VENGEANCE | E. | slowly; carefully; thoughtfully |
| X | 6. TRAWLER | F. | can't be avoided; bound to happen |
| T | 7. IRRITATION | G. | greedy |
| C | 8. INVISIBLE | H. | stuffed with food |
| M | 9. MAULED | I. | the act of chasing or going after something |
| K | 10. INCESSANT | J. | slowly and thoroughly enjoying something |
| F | 11. INEVITABLE | K. | constant |
| G | 12. GLUTTONOUS | L. | a choice or another option |
| S | 13. CEASED | M. | injured by a savage animal attack |
| U | 14. INFERNO | N. | revenge; punishment |
| Q | 15. MONOTONOUS | O. | willfully or disobediently |
| J | 16. SAVORING | P. | total; complete |
| A | 17. DEFIED | Q. | boring; lacking in variety |
| P | 18. UTTER | R. | to move or travel from one place to another |
| D | 19. CONSEQUENCES | S. | stopped |
| R | 20. MIGRATE | T. | annoyance |
| V | 21. VULNERABLE | U. | a very intense fire |
| B | 22. INGENUITY | V. | defenseless and exposed |
| O | 23. DEFIANTLY | W. | very cold; freezing |
| W | 24. FRIGID | X. | a type of fishing boat |
| Y | 25. PERSISTENT | Y. | not giving up; continuing in spite of obstacles |

Touching Spirit Bear Matching 3

1. MIGRATE — A. not able to be seen or noticed
2. MANEUVERED — B. to bear or put up with
3. VULNERABLE — C. hidden or covered
4. INVISIBLE — D. in a threatening manner
5. ANCESTORS — E. twitched or seized
6. ACKNOWLEDGED — F. cleverness
7. INGENUITY — G. in a tired manner
8. MENACINGLY — H. a very intense fire
9. DEFIED — I. family members who have lived before one's own time
10. TRAWLER — J. made fun of
11. MOCKED — K. known to oneself; aware
12. IRKED — L. irritated; annoyed; bothered
13. SHROUDED — M. defenseless and exposed
14. WEARILY — N. very careful; with hesitation; unsure
15. BRANDISHED — O. to move or travel from one place to another
16. SPASMED — P. a vision; figment of the imagination
17. TAUNTED — Q. steered or managed with skill
18. INSIGNIFICANT — R. waved
19. CONSCIOUS — S. not important; meaningless
20. TENTATIVE — T. teased; blamed or scolded in an insulting way
21. HALLUCINATION — U. a feeling of sorrow or remorse
22. BIZARRE — V. strange; weird
23. INFERNO — W. a type of fishing boat
24. ENDURE — X. challenged; boldly resisted or went against
25. REGRET — Y. showed a sign of awareness or acceptance

Touching Spirit Bear Matching 3 Answer Key

| | | | |
|---|---|---|---|
| O | 1. MIGRATE | A. | not able to be seen or noticed |
| Q | 2. MANEUVERED | B. | to bear or put up with |
| M | 3. VULNERABLE | C. | hidden or covered |
| A | 4. INVISIBLE | D. | in a threatening manner |
| I | 5. ANCESTORS | E. | twitched or seized |
| Y | 6. ACKNOWLEDGED | F. | cleverness |
| F | 7. INGENUITY | G. | in a tired manner |
| D | 8. MENACINGLY | H. | a very intense fire |
| X | 9. DEFIED | I. | family members who have lived before one's own time |
| W | 10. TRAWLER | J. | made fun of |
| J | 11. MOCKED | K. | known to oneself; aware |
| L | 12. IRKED | L. | irritated; annoyed; bothered |
| C | 13. SHROUDED | M. | defenseless and exposed |
| G | 14. WEARILY | N. | very careful; with hesitation; unsure |
| R | 15. BRANDISHED | O. | to move or travel from one place to another |
| E | 16. SPASMED | P. | a vision; figment of the imagination |
| T | 17. TAUNTED | Q. | steered or managed with skill |
| S | 18. INSIGNIFICANT | R. | waved |
| K | 19. CONSCIOUS | S. | not important; meaningless |
| N | 20. TENTATIVE | T. | teased; blamed or scolded in an insulting way |
| P | 21. HALLUCINATION | U. | a feeling of sorrow or remorse |
| V | 22. BIZARRE | V. | strange; weird |
| H | 23. INFERNO | W. | a type of fishing boat |
| B | 24. ENDURE | X. | challenged; boldly resisted or went against |
| U | 25. REGRET | Y. | showed a sign of awareness or acceptance |

Touching Spirit Bear Matching 4

1. COMPOSURE
2. STARK
3. DAWDLED
4. OMEN
5. MANIPULATED
6. ENDURE
7. GRUB
8. IRKED
9. DEFIANTLY
10. MONOTONOUS
11. REHABILITATION
12. PURSUIT
13. SCAVENGER
14. ANCESTORS
15. SPASMED
16. IRRITATION
17. UTTER
18. ACKNOWLEDGED
19. INSTINCT
20. MIGRATE
21. INGENUITY
22. VIOLATED
23. HAGGARD
24. INEVITABLE
25. STIFLED

A. annoyance
B. can't be avoided; bound to happen
C. the act of returning to good condition or normalcy
D. showed a sign of awareness or acceptance
E. one who gathers things thrown away by others
F. a sign or warning
G. irritated; annoyed; bothered
H. the act of chasing or going after something
I. family members who have lived before one's own time
J. controlled
K. food
L. cleverness
M. bleak; bare; very plain
N. to move or travel from one place to another
O. calmness
P. wasted time; moved very slowly
Q. withheld; suppressed; ended by force
R. twitched or seized
S. tired-looking; an unhealthy appearance
T. broke a law, rule, agreement, or promise
U. to bear or put up with
V. total; complete
W. willfully or disobediently
X. natural inborn ability
Y. boring; lacking in variety

Touching Spirit Bear Matching 4 Answer Key

| | | | |
|---|---|---|---|
| O | 1. COMPOSURE | A. | annoyance |
| M | 2. STARK | B. | can't be avoided; bound to happen |
| P | 3. DAWDLED | C. | the act of returning to good condition or normalcy |
| F | 4. OMEN | D. | showed a sign of awareness or acceptance |
| J | 5. MANIPULATED | E. | one who gathers things thrown away by others |
| U | 6. ENDURE | F. | a sign or warning |
| K | 7. GRUB | G. | irritated; annoyed; bothered |
| G | 8. IRKED | H. | the act of chasing or going after something |
| W | 9. DEFIANTLY | I. | family members who have lived before one's own time |
| Y | 10. MONOTONOUS | J. | controlled |
| C | 11. REHABILITATION | K. | food |
| H | 12. PURSUIT | L. | cleverness |
| E | 13. SCAVENGER | M. | bleak; bare; very plain |
| I | 14. ANCESTORS | N. | to move or travel from one place to another |
| R | 15. SPASMED | O. | calmness |
| A | 16. IRRITATION | P. | wasted time; moved very slowly |
| V | 17. UTTER | Q. | withheld; suppressed; ended by force |
| D | 18. ACKNOWLEDGED | R. | twitched or seized |
| X | 19. INSTINCT | S. | tired-looking; an unhealthy appearance |
| N | 20. MIGRATE | T. | broke a law, rule, agreement, or promise |
| L | 21. INGENUITY | U. | to bear or put up with |
| T | 22. VIOLATED | V. | total; complete |
| S | 23. HAGGARD | W. | willfully or disobediently |
| B | 24. INEVITABLE | X. | natural inborn ability |
| Q | 25. STIFLED | Y. | boring; lacking in variety |

Touching Spirit Bear Magic Squares 1

Match the definition with the vocabulary word. Put your answers in the magic squares below. When your answers are correct, all columns and rows will add to the same number.

A. HYPNOTIC
B. COMPOSURE
C. VENGEANCE
D. BRANDISHED
E. IRKED
F. BIZARRE
G. STIFLED
H. SARCASM
I. CONSCIOUS
J. ORBS
K. SAVORING
L. ALTERNATIVE
M. SHROUDED
N. DAWDLED
O. VOWED
P. MONOTONOUS

1. calmness
2. withheld; suppressed; ended by force
3. slowly and thoroughly enjoying something
4. wasted time; moved very slowly
5. hidden or covered
6. a choice or another option
7. the use of words to express bitterness or mockery; scorn
8. fascinating; having a sleep-inducing effect
9. boring; lacking in variety
10. known to oneself; aware
11. irritated; annoyed; bothered
12. waved
13. revenge; punishment
14. strange; weird
15. round objects
16. promised; pledged

| A= | B= | C= | D= |
|---|---|---|---|
| E= | F= | G= | H= |
| I= | J= | K= | L= |
| M= | N= | O= | P= |

Touching Spirit Bear Magic Squares 1 Answer Key

Match the definition with the vocabulary word. Put your answers in the magic squares below. When your answers are correct, all columns and rows will add to the same number.

A. HYPNOTIC
B. COMPOSURE
C. VENGEANCE
D. BRANDISHED
E. IRKED
F. BIZARRE
G. STIFLED
H. SARCASM
I. CONSCIOUS
J. ORBS
K. SAVORING
L. ALTERNATIVE
M. SHROUDED
N. DAWDLED
O. VOWED
P. MONOTONOUS

1. calmness
2. withheld; suppressed; ended by force
3. slowly and thoroughly enjoying something
4. wasted time; moved very slowly
5. hidden or covered
6. a choice or another option
7. the use of words to express bitterness or mockery; scorn
8. fascinating; having a sleep-inducing effect
9. boring; lacking in variety
10. known to oneself; aware
11. irritated; annoyed; bothered
12. waved
13. revenge; punishment
14. strange; weird
15. round objects
16. promised; pledged

| A=8 | B=1 | C=13 | D=12 |
|---|---|---|---|
| E=11 | F=14 | G=2 | H=7 |
| I=10 | J=15 | K=3 | L=6 |
| M=5 | N=4 | O=16 | P=9 |

Touching Spirit Bear Magic Squares 2

Match the definition with the vocabulary word. Put your answers in the magic squares below. When your answers are correct, all columns and rows will add to the same number.

A. CONJURING
B. BANISHMENT
C. HYPNOTIC
D. MONOTONOUS
E. BRANDISHED
F. STARK
G. GRIMACING
H. INGENUITY
I. IMPATIENT
J. PURSUIT
K. FEIGNED
L. FESTER
M. TREACHEROUS
N. FREQUENT
O. CONSCIOUS
P. WEARILY

1. bringing to mind; recalling
2. often
3. the act of chasing or going after something
4. waved
5. making a facial expression that indicates disapproval, pain, or difficulty
6. to become an irritating, infected, sore spot
7. in a tired manner
8. fascinating; having a sleep-inducing effect
9. known to oneself; aware
10. boring; lacking in variety
11. cleverness
12. pretended
13. unable to wait; not accepting delay
14. bleak; bare; very plain
15. removal from society; exile
16. dangerous; hazardous

| A= | B= | C= | D= |
| E= | F= | G= | H= |
| I= | J= | K= | L= |
| M= | N= | O= | P= |

Touching Spirit Bear Magic Squares 2 Answer Key

Match the definition with the vocabulary word. Put your answers in the magic squares below. When your answers are correct, all columns and rows will add to the same number.

A. CONJURING          E. BRANDISHED        I. IMPATIENT         M. TREACHEROUS
B. BANISHMENT         F. STARK             J. PURSUIT           N. FREQUENT
C. HYPNOTIC           G. GRIMACING         K. FEIGNED           O. CONSCIOUS
D. MONOTONOUS         H. INGENUITY         L. FESTER            P. WEARILY

1. bringing to mind; recalling
2. often
3. the act of chasing or going after something
4. waved
5. making a facial expression that indicates disapproval, pain, or difficulty
6. to become an irritating, infected, sore spot
7. in a tired manner
8. fascinating; having a sleep-inducing effect
9. known to oneself; aware
10. boring; lacking in variety
11. cleverness
12. pretended
13. unable to wait; not accepting delay
14. bleak; bare; very plain
15. removal from society; exile
16. dangerous; hazardous

| A=1  | B=15 | C=8  | D=10 |
| E=4  | F=14 | G=5  | H=11 |
| I=13 | J=3  | K=12 | L=6  |
| M=16 | N=2  | O=9  | P=7  |

Touching Spirit Bear Magic Squares 3

Match the definition with the vocabulary word. Put your answers in the magic squares below. When your answers are correct, all columns and rows will add to the same number.

A. DEFIED
B. POTENTIAL
C. FRIGID
D. MAULED
E. IRRITATION
F. TENTATIVE
G. SPASMED
H. GLUTTONOUS
I. OMEN
J. ENDURE
K. RELINQUISH
L. TRANCE
M. ORBS
N. REHABILITATION
O. DEFIANTLY
P. FEIGNED

1. the ability or capability
2. twitched or seized
3. to release or surrender
4. the act of returning to good condition or normalcy
5. round objects
6. the state of being semi-aware; in a daze
7. greedy
8. challenged; boldly resisted or went against
9. pretended
10. a sign or warning
11. annoyance
12. injured by a savage animal attack
13. very cold; freezing
14. very careful; with hesitation; unsure
15. to bear or put up with
16. willfully or disobediently

| A= | B= | C= | D= |
| E= | F= | G= | H= |
| I= | J= | K= | L= |
| M= | N= | O= | P= |

Touching Spirit Bear Magic Squares 3 Answer Key

Match the definition with the vocabulary word. Put your answers in the magic squares below. When your answers are correct, all columns and rows will add to the same number.

A. DEFIED
B. POTENTIAL
C. FRIGID
D. MAULED
E. IRRITATION
F. TENTATIVE
G. SPASMED
H. GLUTTONOUS
I. OMEN
J. ENDURE
K. RELINQUISH
L. TRANCE
M. ORBS
N. REHABILITATION
O. DEFIANTLY
P. FEIGNED

1. the ability or capability
2. twitched or seized
3. to release or surrender
4. the act of returning to good condition or normalcy
5. round objects
6. the state of being semi-aware; in a daze
7. greedy
8. challenged; boldly resisted or went against
9. pretended
10. a sign or warning
11. annoyance
12. injured by a savage animal attack
13. very cold; freezing
14. very careful; with hesitation; unsure
15. to bear or put up with
16. willfully or disobediently

| A=8 | B=1 | C=13 | D=12 |
|---|---|---|---|
| E=11 | F=14 | G=2 | H=7 |
| I=10 | J=15 | K=3 | L=6 |
| M=5 | N=4 | O=16 | P=9 |

Touching Spirit Bear Magic Squares 4

Match the definition with the vocabulary word. Put your answers in the magic squares below. When your answers are correct, all columns and rows will add to the same number.

A. RELUCTANTLY
B. WARILY
C. OMEN
D. FRIGID
E. MIGRATE
F. VENGEANCE
G. TRAUMA
H. POTENTIAL
I. FESTER
J. VIOLATED
K. CEASED
L. COMPOSURE
M. INFERNO
N. IMPATIENT
O. DEFIANTLY
P. INGENUITY

1. the ability or capability
2. unwillingly; with hesitation
3. cautiously
4. painful damage
5. broke a law, rule, agreement, or promise
6. willfully or disobediently
7. cleverness
8. to become an irritating, infected, sore spot
9. stopped
10. unable to wait; not accepting delay
11. a very intense fire
12. calmness
13. to move or travel from one place to another
14. very cold; freezing
15. a sign or warning
16. revenge; punishment

| A= | B= | C= | D= |
| E= | F= | G= | H= |
| I= | J= | K= | L= |
| M= | N= | O= | P= |

Touching Spirit Bear Magic Squares 4 Answer Key

Match the definition with the vocabulary word. Put your answers in the magic squares below. When your answers are correct, all columns and rows will add to the same number.

A. RELUCTANTLY
B. WARILY
C. OMEN
D. FRIGID
E. MIGRATE
F. VENGEANCE
G. TRAUMA
H. POTENTIAL
I. FESTER
J. VIOLATED
K. CEASED
L. COMPOSURE
M. INFERNO
N. IMPATIENT
O. DEFIANTLY
P. INGENUITY

1. the ability or capability
2. unwillingly; with hesitation
3. cautiously
4. painful damage
5. broke a law, rule, agreement, or promise
6. willfully or disobediently
7. cleverness
8. to become an irritating, infected, sore spot
9. stopped
10. unable to wait; not accepting delay
11. a very intense fire
12. calmness
13. to move or travel from one place to another
14. very cold; freezing
15. a sign or warning
16. revenge; punishment

| A=2 | B=3 | C=15 | D=14 |
|---|---|---|---|
| E=13 | F=16 | G=4 | H=1 |
| I=8 | J=5 | K=9 | L=12 |
| M=11 | N=10 | O=6 | P=7 |

# Touching Spirit Bear Word Search 1

Words are placed backwards, forward, diagonally, up and down. Clues listed below can help you find the words. Circle the hidden vocabulary words in the maze.

```
R  E  V  E  R  E  N  T  L  Y  I  O  G  I  P
F  E  S  T  E  R  G  C  W  H  D  R  K  N  E
B  C  D  P  H  V  X  N  A  H  U  B  K  F  R
D  N  W  E  V  B  R  I  R  B  I  S  F  E  U
F  A  C  M  M  U  Y  T  I  Q  N  A  E  R  D
V  R  V  O  T  P  L  S  L  M  E  R  I  N  N
E  T  I  N  M  L  T  N  Y  D  V  C  G  O  E
Z  W  O  O  F  P  C  I  E  N  I  A  N  G  S
I  I  L  T  R  X  O  R  O  R  T  S  E  N  D
R  N  A  O  I  R  E  S  V  N  A  M  D  E  E
E  C  T  N  G  V  K  O  U  V  B  B  S  O  G
M  I  E  O  I  Y  W  Q  S  R  L  A  L  M  R
S  N  D  U  D  E  G  R  E  M  E  S  J  E  O
E  G  Q  S  D  D  D  E  K  C  O  M  C  N  G
M  A  U  L  E  D  I  N  G  E  N  U  I  T  Y
```

a sign or warning (4)
a very intense fire (7)
boring; lacking in variety (10)
broke a law, rule, agreement, or promise (8)
calmness (9)
came out (7)
can't be avoided; bound to happen (10)
cautiously (6)
cleverness (9)
defenseless and exposed (10)
drawing back or tensing the body or face (7)
food (4)
forgiveness through making up for a wrongdoing (10)
injured by a savage animal attack (6)
irritated; annoyed; bothered (5)
made fun of (6)
natural inborn ability (8)
pretended (7)
promised; pledged (5)
respectfully (10)
round objects (4)
stopped (6)
stuffed with food (6)
the state of being semi-aware; in a daze (6)
the use of words to express bitterness or mockery; scorn (7)
to bear or put up with (6)
to become an irritating, infected, sore spot (6)
to put into a trance; bewitch (9)
trembled; vibrated (8)
very cold; freezing (6)

Touching Spirit Bear Word Search 1 Answer Key

Words are placed backwards, forward, diagonally, up and down. Clues listed below can help you find the words. Circle the hidden vocabulary words in the maze.

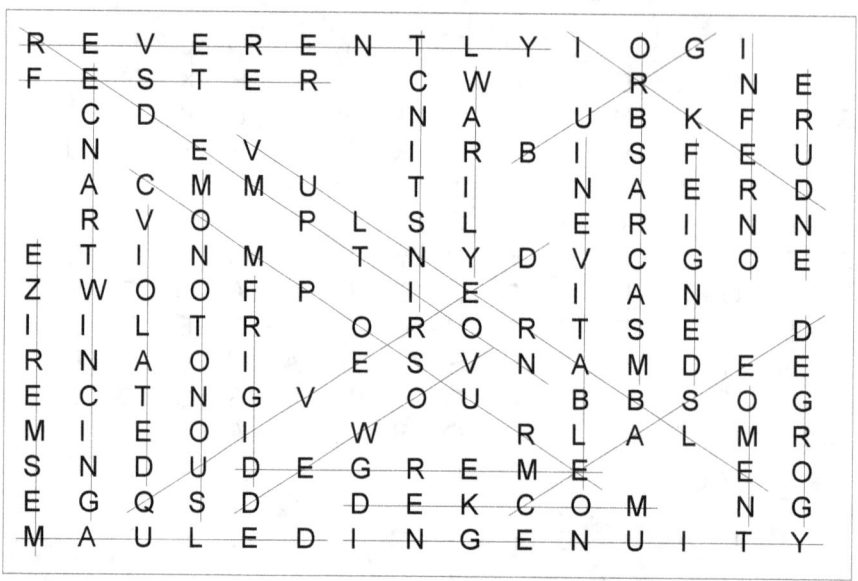

a sign or warning (4)
a very intense fire (7)
boring; lacking in variety (10)
broke a law, rule, agreement, or promise (8)
calmness (9)
came out (7)
can't be avoided; bound to happen (10)
cautiously (6)
cleverness (9)
defenseless and exposed (10)
drawing back or tensing the body or face (7)
food (4)
forgiveness through making up for a wrongdoing (10)
injured by a savage animal attack (6)
irritated; annoyed; bothered (5)
made fun of (6)
natural inborn ability (8)
pretended (7)
promised; pledged (5)
respectfully (10)
round objects (4)
stopped (6)
stuffed with food (6)
the state of being semi-aware; in a daze (6)
the use of words to express bitterness or mockery; scorn (7)
to bear or put up with (6)
to become an irritating, infected, sore spot (6)
to put into a trance; bewitch (9)
trembled; vibrated (8)
very cold; freezing (6)

# Touching Spirit Bear Word Search 2

Words are placed backwards, forward, diagonally, up and down. Clues listed below can help you find the words. Circle the hidden vocabulary words in the maze.

```
S C A V E N G E R F S F T M Y
T E R G E R R M S R P E R O K
I R E T T U Y E A I A S A C W
F P S C D L R R V G S T N K R
L Z C N I P Y G O I M E C E Y
E P E R S V L E R D E R E D S
D N A V B I M D I V D D G D Z
S W Y D F O Z I N D E G R O G
T H X J R L Z T G L N J N S T
R I R Y E A P L D R D R T O G
A G R O Q T H W V E A A O R Z
U T F K U E A D S O R T M B Z
M A U L E D R A W K W A E S H
A W Y C N D E R E V U E N A M
K K W J T C Z D G R U B D D Y
```

a feeling of sorrow or remorse (6)
a sign or warning (4)
bleak; bare; very plain (5)
broke a law, rule, agreement, or promise (8)
came out (7)
cautiously (6)
food (4)
hidden or covered (8)
inconvenient; difficult; uncomfortable; clumsy (7)
injured by a savage animal attack (6)
irritated; annoyed; bothered (5)
made fun of (6)
often (8)
one who gathers things thrown away by others (9)
painful damage (6)
promised; pledged (5)
round objects (4)
slowly and thoroughly enjoying something (8)
steered or managed with skill (10)
stopped (6)
stuffed with food (6)
the state of being semi-aware; in a daze (6)
to bear or put up with (6)
to become an irritating, infected, sore spot (6)
to move or travel from one place to another (7)
total; complete (5)
twitched or seized (7)
very cold; freezing (6)
wasted time; moved very slowly (7)
withheld; suppressed; ended by force (7)

Touching Spirit Bear Word Search 2 Answer Key

Words are placed backwards, forward, diagonally, up and down. Clues listed below can help you find the words. Circle the hidden vocabulary words in the maze.

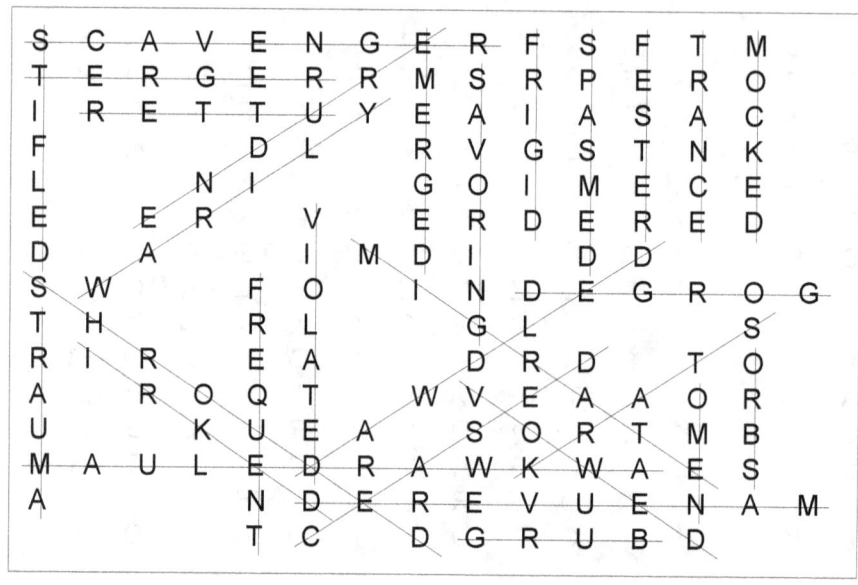

a feeling of sorrow or remorse (6)
a sign or warning (4)
bleak; bare; very plain (5)
broke a law, rule, agreement, or promise (8)
came out (7)
cautiously (6)
food (4)
hidden or covered (8)
inconvenient; difficult; uncomfortable; clumsy (7)
injured by a savage animal attack (6)
irritated; annoyed; bothered (5)
made fun of (6)
often (8)
one who gathers things thrown away by others (9)
painful damage (6)

promised; pledged (5)
round objects (4)
slowly and thoroughly enjoying something (8)
steered or managed with skill (10)
stopped (6)
stuffed with food (6)
the state of being semi-aware; in a daze (6)
to bear or put up with (6)
to become an irritating, infected, sore spot (6)
to move or travel from one place to another (7)
total; complete (5)
twitched or seized (7)
very cold; freezing (6)
wasted time; moved very slowly (7)
withheld; suppressed; ended by force (7)

# Touching Spirit Bear Word Search 3

Words are placed backwards, forward, diagonally, up and down. Words listed below are included in the maze. Circle the hidden vocabulary words in the maze.

```
F A T B W X M D E D U O R H S
P R L R W A P O W F E G R Z R
N A E T A C R P C T E F R B W
J W C Q E U O I J K V S I U S
K K M O U R M A L E E O T E B
B W A V N E N A X Y N D W E D
R A U U Y J N A S I M D R E R
A R L L G L U T T O N O U S D
N D E N G C C R M I R G H R F
D C D E T A L O I V V A G D E
I D E R E V I U Q N G E C E I
S P S A V O R I N G G B O G G
H M H B S T K R A T S G M R N
E B R L X E E R E T T U E O E
D J R E G R D W I N C I N G D
```

ALTERNATIVE     FEIGNED     MAULED     TRAUMA
AWKWARD     FESTER     MOCKED     UTTER
BRANDISHED     FREQUENT     OMEN     VIOLATED
CEASED     GLUTTONOUS     ORBS     VOWED
COAXING     GORGED     QUIVERED     VULNERABLE
CONJURING     GRUB     SAVORING     WARILY
DEFIED     HAGGARD     SHROUDED     WINCING
ENDURE     IRKED     STARK

Touching Spirit Bear Word Search 3 Answer Key

Words are placed backwards, forward, diagonally, up and down. Words listed below are included in the maze. Circle the hidden vocabulary words in the maze.

| ALTERNATIVE | FEIGNED | MAULED | TRAUMA |
| AWKWARD | FESTER | MOCKED | UTTER |
| BRANDISHED | FREQUENT | OMEN | VIOLATED |
| CEASED | GLUTTONOUS | ORBS | VOWED |
| COAXING | GORGED | QUIVERED | VULNERABLE |
| CONJURING | GRUB | SAVORING | WARILY |
| DEFIED | HAGGARD | SHROUDED | WINCING |
| ENDURE | IRKED | STARK | |

# Touching Spirit Bear Word Search 4

Words are placed backwards, forward, diagonally, up and down. Words listed below are included in the maze. Circle the hidden vocabulary words in the maze.

```
H A L L U C I N A T I O N A E
S G W H W R E G Y R N V N Z R
T O C P K M N R R G C F M U
A R R E O I A I E D E F I E D
R G D S X T T F K S N R S S N
K E Z A I A N T T W U E C M E
H D O L T I C O F S I Q A E F
Y C O I Z N R U E A T U V R R
P S O D I S P T S R Y E E I I
N N X T S R A T T C C N N Z G
O S S F J R W E E A S T G E I
T N X L G G H R R S Y G E T D
I N V I S I B L E M S B R O H
C H M C S P A S M E D H D U Q
C O N J U R I N G V O W E D B
```

| ANCESTORS | GORGED | IRKED | SOLITARY |
| COAXING | GRUB | IRRITATION | SPASMED |
| CONJURING | HALLUCINATION | MESMERIZE | STARK |
| DEFIED | HYPNOTIC | MIGRATE | UTTER |
| ENDURE | INFERNO | OMEN | VOWED |
| FESTER | INGENUITY | ORBS | |
| FREQUENT | INSTINCT | SARCASM | |
| FRIGID | INVISIBLE | SCAVENGER | |

Touching Spirit Bear Word Search 4 Answer Key

Words are placed backwards, forward, diagonally, up and down. Words listed below are included in the maze. Circle the hidden vocabulary words in the maze.

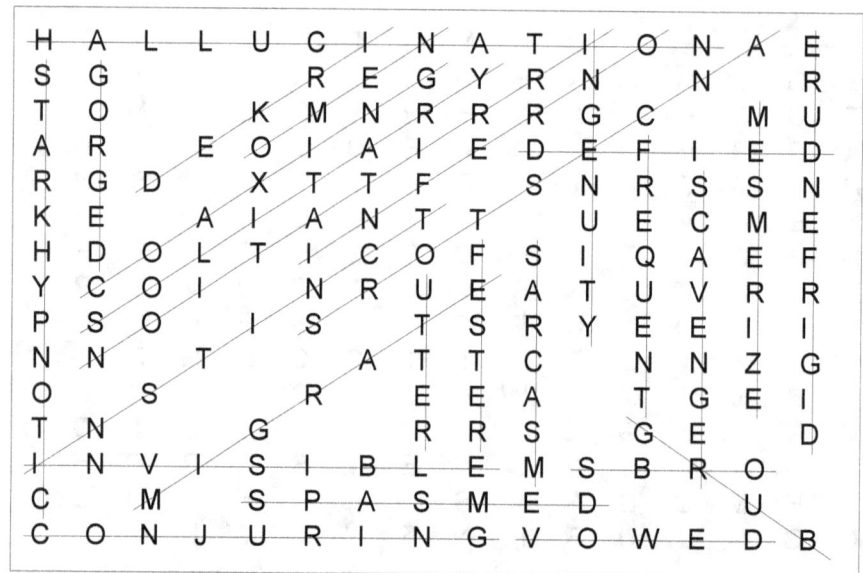

| ANCESTORS | GORGED | IRKED | SOLITARY |
| COAXING | GRUB | IRRITATION | SPASMED |
| CONJURING | HALLUCINATION | MESMERIZE | STARK |
| DEFIED | HYPNOTIC | MIGRATE | UTTER |
| ENDURE | INFERNO | OMEN | VOWED |
| FESTER | INGENUITY | ORBS | |
| FREQUENT | INSTINCT | SARCASM | |
| FRIGID | INVISIBLE | SCAVENGER | |

Touching Spirit Bear Crossword 1

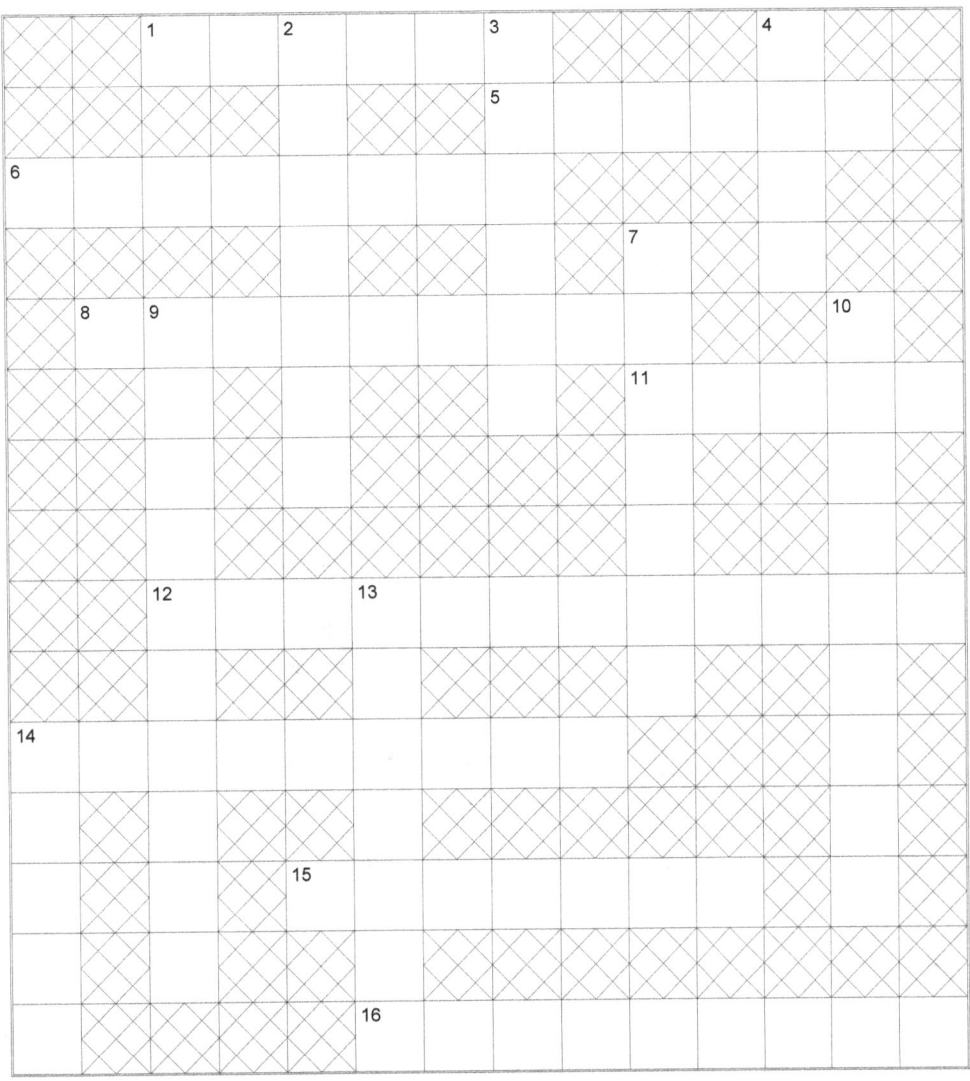

Across
1. to become an irritating, infected, sore spot
5. to bear or put up with
6. slowly and thoroughly enjoying something
8. unable to wait; not accepting delay
11. irritated; annoyed; bothered
12. effects or results
14. revenge; punishment
15. came out
16. willfully or disobediently

Down
2. the use of words to express bitterness or mockery; scorn
3. a feeling of sorrow or remorse
4. food
7. withheld; suppressed; ended by force
9. in a threatening manner
10. to put into a trance; bewitch
13. twitched or seized
14. promised; pledged

Touching Spirit Bear Crossword 1 Answer Key

|   |   | 1 F | E | 2 S | T | E | 3 R |   |   | 4 G |   |   |
|---|---|---|---|---|---|---|---|---|---|---|---|---|
|   |   |   |   | A |   |   | 5 E | N | D | U | R | E |
| 6 S | A | V | O | R | I | N | G |   |   | U |   |   |
|   |   |   |   | C |   |   | R |   | 7 S | B |   |   |
|   |   | 8 | 9 M | P | A | T | I | E | N | T |   | 10 M |
|   |   |   | E | S |   |   | T |   | 11 I | R | K | E | D |
|   |   |   | N | M |   |   |   |   | F |   |   | S |
|   |   |   | A |   |   |   |   |   | L |   |   | M |
|   |   |   | 12 C | O | N | 13 S | E | Q | U | E | N | C | E | S |
|   |   |   | I |   |   | P |   |   | D |   |   | R |
| 14 V | E | N | G | E | A | N | C | E |   |   |   | I |
| O |   |   | G |   |   | S |   |   |   |   |   | Z |
| W |   |   | L |   | 15 E | M | E | R | G | E | D | E |
| E |   |   | Y |   | E |   |   |   |   |   |   |   |
| D |   |   |   |   | 16 D | E | F | I | A | N | T | L | Y |

Across
1. to become an irritating, infected, sore spot
5. to bear or put up with
6. slowly and thoroughly enjoying something
8. unable to wait; not accepting delay
11. irritated; annoyed; bothered
12. effects or results
14. revenge; punishment
15. came out
16. willfully or disobediently

Down
2. the use of words to express bitterness or mockery; scorn
3. a feeling of sorrow or remorse
4. food
7. withheld; suppressed; ended by force
9. in a threatening manner
10. to put into a trance; bewitch
13. twitched or seized
14. promised; pledged

Touching Spirit Bear Crossword 2

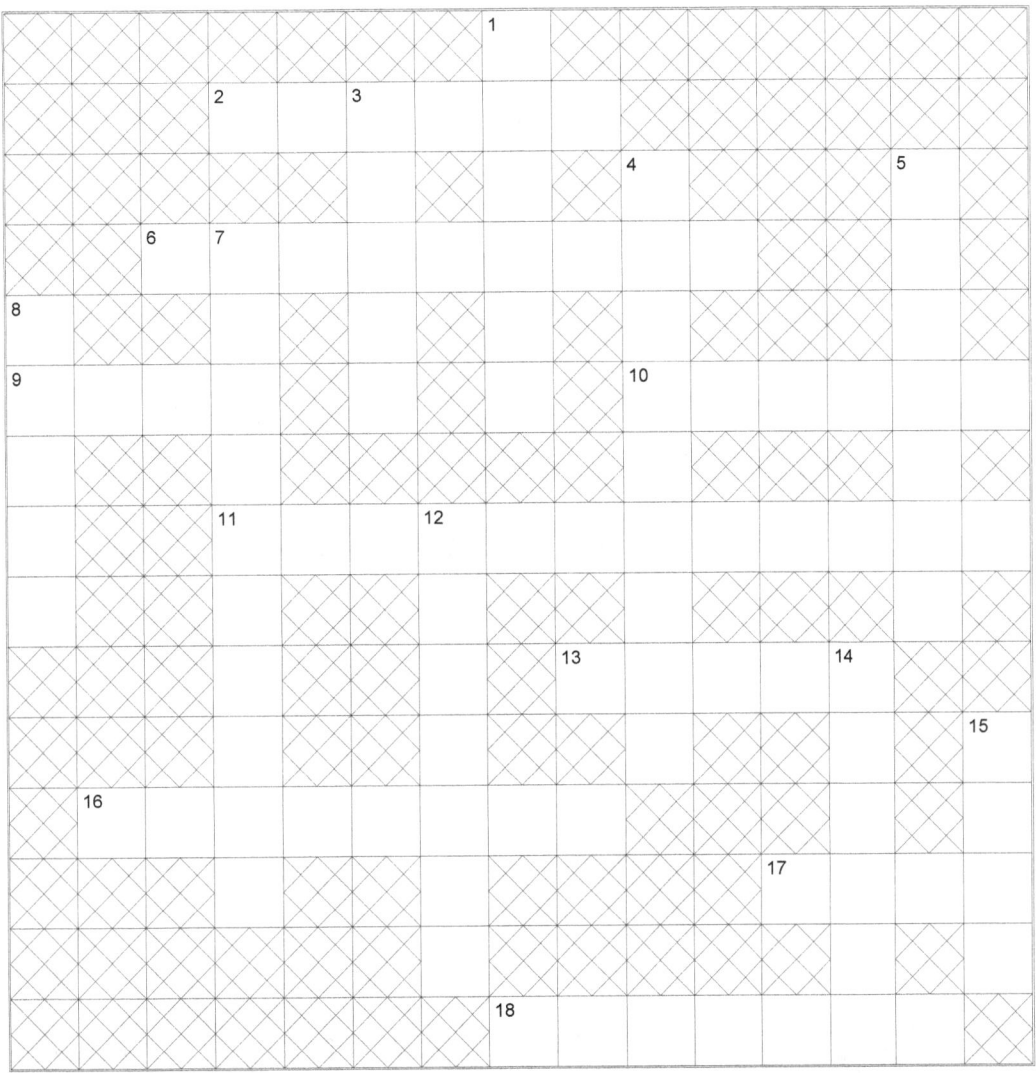

Across
2. to become an irritating, infected, sore spot
6. unable to wait; not accepting delay
9. a sign or warning
10. to bear or put up with
11. effects or results
13. total; complete
16. alone; singular
17. food
18. to move or travel from one place to another

Down
1. challenged; boldly resisted or went against
3. bleak; bare; very plain
4. cleverness
5. came out
7. in a threatening manner
8. promised; pledged
12. the use of words to express bitterness or mockery; scorn
14. a feeling of sorrow or remorse
15. round objects

Touching Spirit Bear Crossword 2 Answer Key

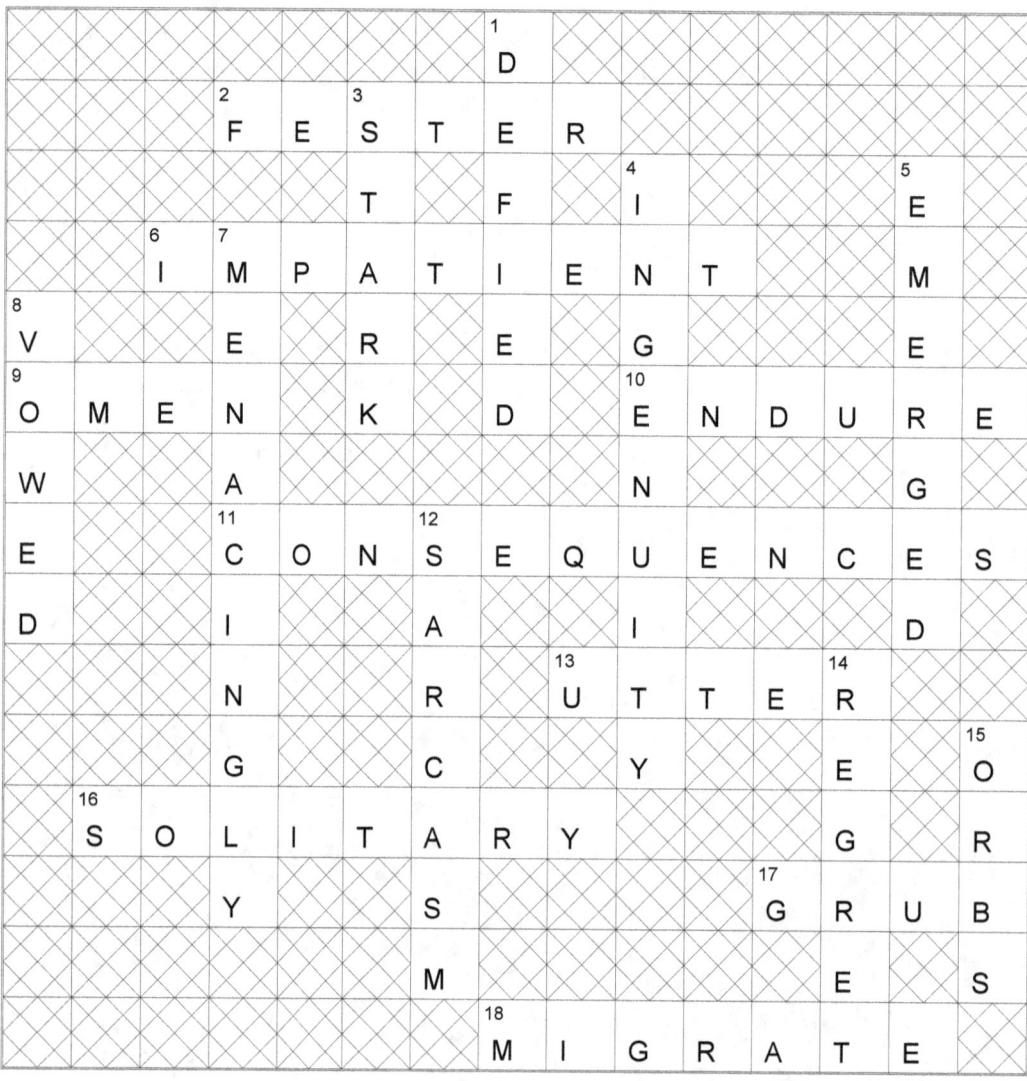

Across
2. to become an irritating, infected, sore spot
6. unable to wait; not accepting delay
9. a sign or warning
10. to bear or put up with
11. effects or results
13. total; complete
16. alone; singular
17. food
18. to move or travel from one place to another

Down
1. challenged; boldly resisted or went against
3. bleak; bare; very plain
4. cleverness
5. came out
7. in a threatening manner
8. promised; pledged
12. the use of words to express bitterness or mockery; scorn
14. a feeling of sorrow or remorse
15. round objects

Touching Spirit Bear Crossword 3

Across
1. to become an irritating, infected, sore spot
4. a sign or warning
6. unable to wait; not accepting delay
8. to bear or put up with
10. effects or results
12. total; complete
15. alone; singular
16. food
18. to move or travel from one place to another
19. twitched or seized

Down
2. bleak; bare; very plain
3. cleverness
5. came out
7. in a threatening manner
9. family members who have lived before one's own time
11. the use of words to express bitterness or mockery; scorn
13. a feeling of sorrow or remorse
14. teased; blamed or scolded in an insulting way
17. round objects

Touching Spirit Bear Crossword 3 Answer Key

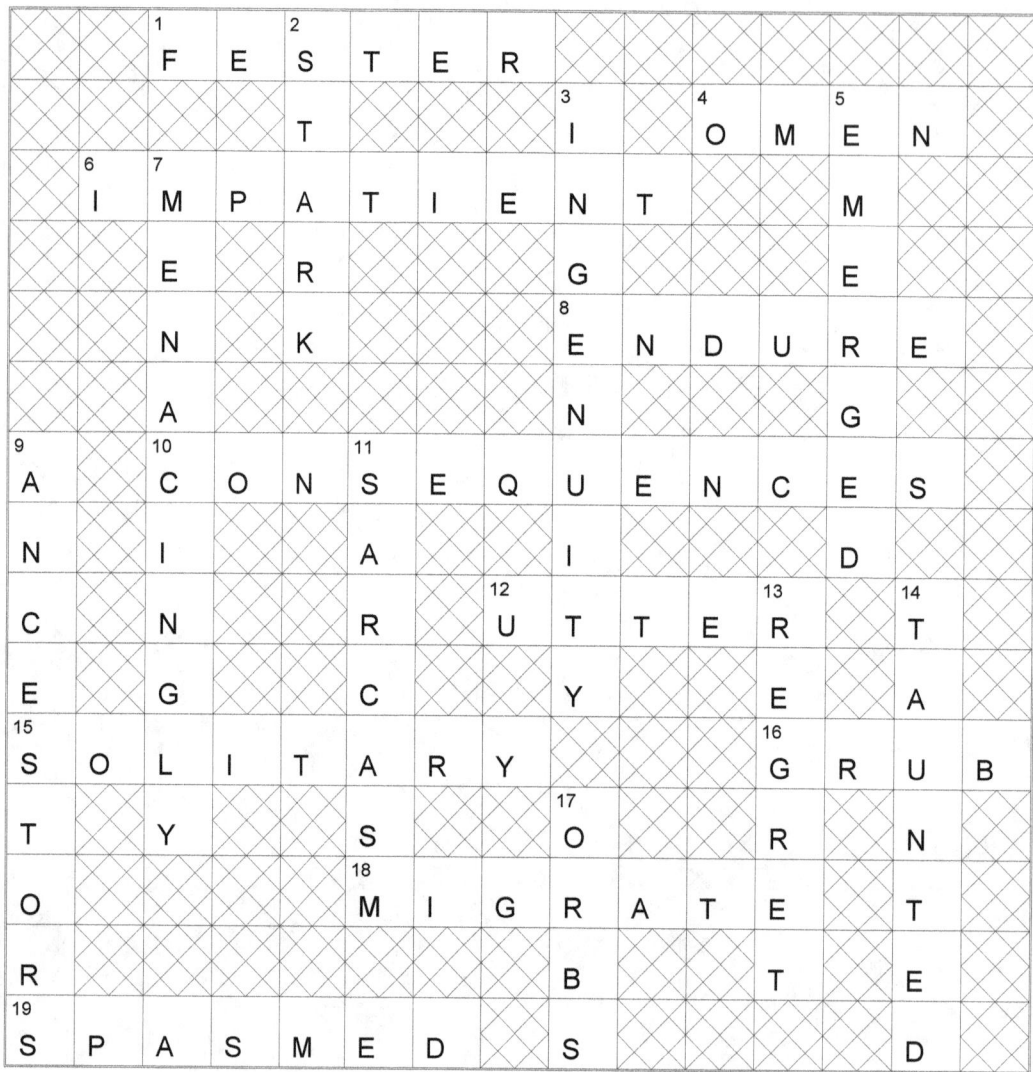

Across
1. to become an irritating, infected, sore spot
4. a sign or warning
6. unable to wait; not accepting delay
8. to bear or put up with
10. effects or results
12. total; complete
15. alone; singular
16. food
18. to move or travel from one place to another
19. twitched or seized

Down
2. bleak; bare; very plain
3. cleverness
5. came out
7. in a threatening manner
9. family members who have lived before one's own time
11. the use of words to express bitterness or mockery; scorn
13. a feeling of sorrow or remorse
14. teased; blamed or scolded in an insulting way
17. round objects

# Touching Spirit Bear Crossword 4

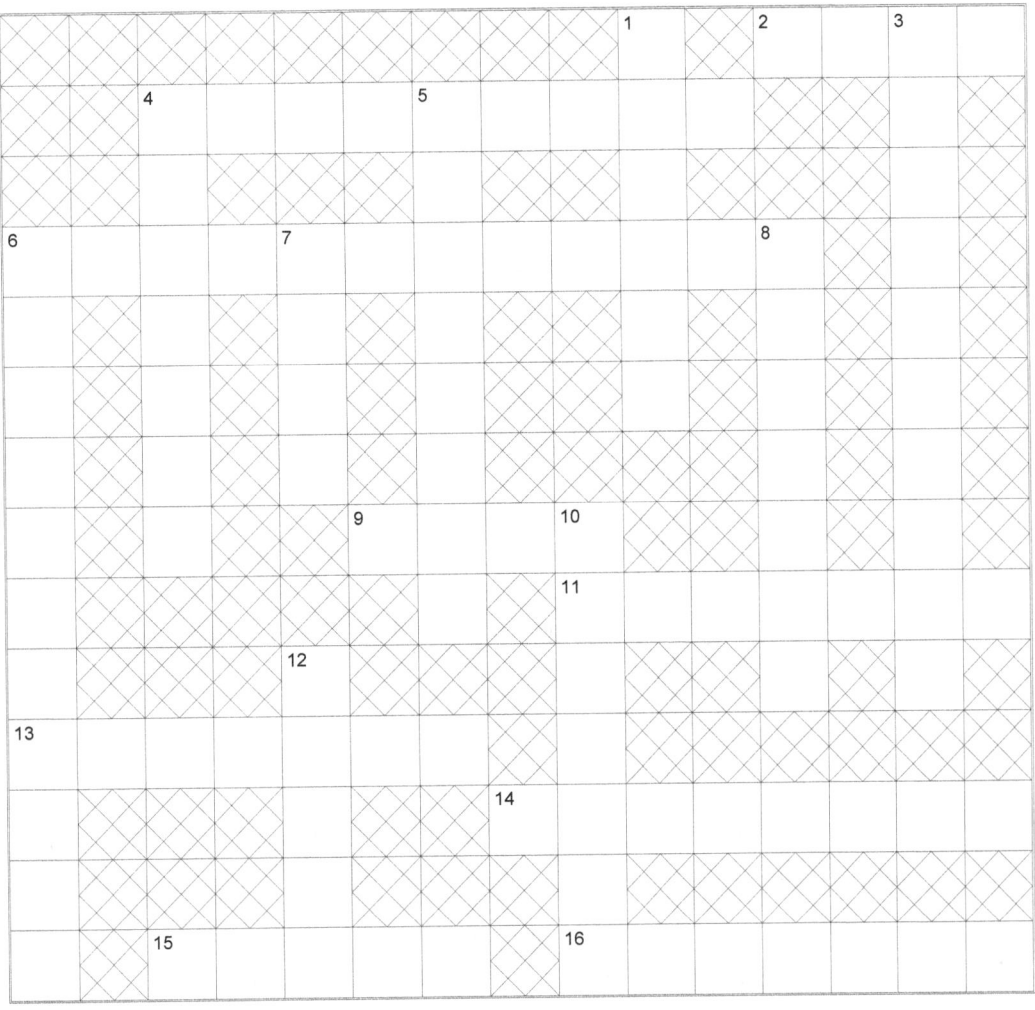

**Across**
2. round objects
4. family members who have lived before one's own time
6. showed a sign of awareness or acceptance
9. food
11. a very intense fire
13. teased; blamed or scolded in an insulting way
14. often
15. irritated; annoyed; bothered
16. came out

**Down**
1. very cold; freezing
3. removal from society; exile
4. inconvenient; difficult; uncomfortable; clumsy
5. alone; singular
6. a choice or another option
7. a sign or warning
8. wasted time; moved very slowly
10. strange; weird
12. bleak; bare; very plain

Touching Spirit Bear Crossword 4 Answer Key

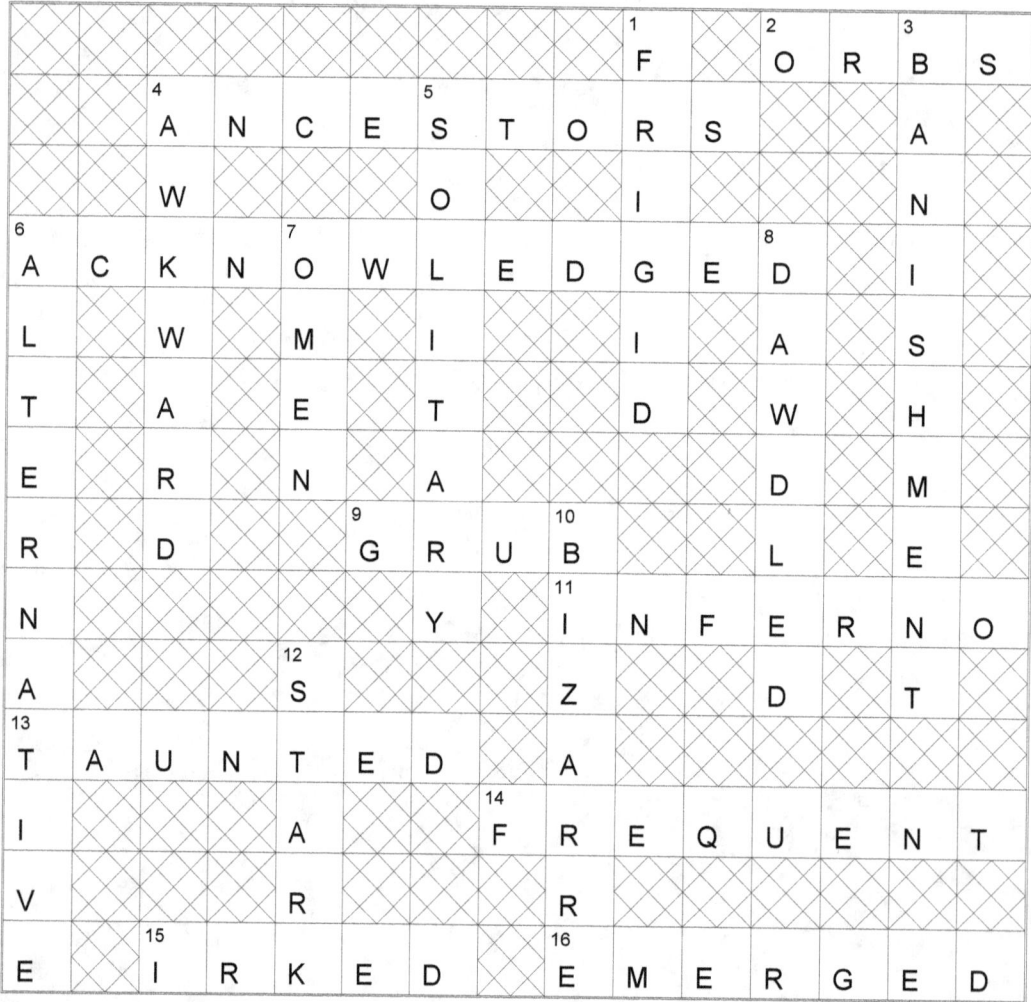

Across
2. round objects
4. family members who have lived before one's own time
6. showed a sign of awareness or acceptance
9. food
11. a very intense fire
13. teased; blamed or scolded in an insulting way
14. often
15. irritated; annoyed; bothered
16. came out

Down
1. very cold; freezing
3. removal from society; exile
4. inconvenient; difficult; uncomfortable; clumsy
5. alone; singular
6. a choice or another option
7. a sign or warning
8. wasted time; moved very slowly
10. strange; weird
12. bleak; bare; very plain

Touching Spirit Bear Juggle Letters 1

_____   = 1. SBOR
                      round objects

_____   = 2. IXCONGA
                      gentle attempts to persuade or influence

_____   = 3. WDLEDDA
                      wasted time; moved very slowly

_____   = 4. ATAMUR
                      painful damage

_____   = 5. NTVEATIET
                      very careful; with hesitation; unsure

_____   = 6. QEUENSOESNCC
                      effects or results

_____   = 7. ENTYNUIGI
                      cleverness

_____   = 8. TTAMIEIPN
                      unable to wait; not accepting delay

_____   = 9. RASTK
                      bleak; bare; very plain

_____   =10. DEOGGR
                      stuffed with food

_____   =11. ARLRWTE
                      a type of fishing boat

_____   =12. FEINYLADT
                      willfully or disobediently

_____   =13. GHDGRAA
                      tired-looking; an unhealthy appearance

_____   =14. AIYBEELLTDER
                      slowly; carefully; thoughtfully

_____   =15. SUREOCPMO
                      calmness

Touching Spirit Bear Juggle Letters 1 Answer Key

ORBS = 1. SBOR
round objects

COAXING = 2. IXCONGA
gentle attempts to persuade or influence

DAWDLED = 3. WDLEDDA
wasted time; moved very slowly

TRAUMA = 4. ATAMUR
painful damage

TENTATIVE = 5. NTVEATIET
very careful; with hesitation; unsure

CONSEQUENCES = 6. QEUENSOESNCC
effects or results

INGENUITY = 7. ENTYNUIGI
cleverness

IMPATIENT = 8. TTAMIEIPN
unable to wait; not accepting delay

STARK = 9. RASTK
bleak; bare; very plain

GORGED = 10. DEOGGR
stuffed with food

TRAWLER = 11. ARLRWTE
a type of fishing boat

DEFIANTLY = 12. FEINYLADT
willfully or disobediently

HAGGARD = 13. GHDGRAA
tired-looking; an unhealthy appearance

DELIBERATELY = 14. AIYBEELLTDER
slowly; carefully; thoughtfully

COMPOSURE = 15. SUREOCPMO
calmness

# Touching Spirit Bear Juggle Letters 2

_____ = 1. EERSZEMMI
   to put into a trance; bewitch

_____ = 2. DNEIGEF
   pretended

_____ = 3. EOUNSQENSCCE
   effects or results

_____ = 4. GRNJOCINU
   bringing to mind; recalling

_____ = 5. VSOANGIR
   slowly and thoroughly enjoying something

_____ = 6. IIETMAPTN
   unable to wait; not accepting delay

_____ = 7. GAARGHD
   tired-looking; an unhealthy appearance

_____ = 8. RTSEFE
   to become an irritating, infected, sore spot

_____ = 9. KREID
   irritated; annoyed; bothered

_____ =10. TNOGLTUSOU
   greedy

_____ =11. GFRDII
   very cold; freezing

_____ =12. UBGR
   food

_____ =13. EMRNAUEEDV
   steered or managed with skill

_____ =14. RITAONITRI
   annoyance

_____ =15. MDPSAES
   twitched or seized

Touching Spirit Bear Juggle Letters 2 Answer Key

MESMERIZE = 1. EERSZEMMI
to put into a trance; bewitch

FEIGNED = 2. DNEIGEF
pretended

CONSEQUENCES = 3. EOUNSQENSCCE
effects or results

CONJURING = 4. GRNJOCINU
bringing to mind; recalling

SAVORING = 5. VSOANGIR
slowly and thoroughly enjoying something

IMPATIENT = 6. IIETMAPTN
unable to wait; not accepting delay

HAGGARD = 7. GAARGHD
tired-looking; an unhealthy appearance

FESTER = 8. RTSEFE
to become an irritating, infected, sore spot

IRKED = 9. KREID
irritated; annoyed; bothered

GLUTTONOUS = 10. TNOGLTUSOU
greedy

FRIGID = 11. GFRDII
very cold; freezing

GRUB = 12. UBGR
food

MANEUVERED = 13. EMRNAUEEDV
steered or managed with skill

IRRITATION = 14. RITAONITRI
annoyance

SPASMED = 15. MDPSAES
twitched or seized

Touching Spirit Bear Juggle Letters 3

_____ = 1. ETCRNA
the state of being semi-aware; in a daze

_____ = 2. USNOOUGTLT
greedy

_____ = 3. OREEHARCUTS
dangerous; hazardous

_____ = 4. IHUAIONTLCLAN
a vision; figment of the imagination

_____ = 5. RAEBRZI
strange; weird

_____ = 6. IDLEVAOT
broke a law, rule, agreement, or promise

_____ = 7. ABEVULNLER
defenseless and exposed

_____ = 8. DRIEUVQE
trembled; vibrated

_____ = 9. GRETER
a feeling of sorrow or remorse

_____ =10. NTRDIEPEOM
forgiveness through making up for a wrongdoing

_____ =11. EAUDLM
injured by a savage animal attack

_____ =12. TEPDILAMUAN
controlled

_____ =13. DAGRHGA
tired-looking; an unhealthy appearance

_____ =14. VBIILEINS
not able to be seen or noticed

_____ =15. AOVGNSRI
slowly and thoroughly enjoying something

Touching Spirit Bear Juggle Letters 3 Answer Key

TRANCE = 1. ETCRNA
the state of being semi-aware; in a daze

GLUTTONOUS = 2. USNOOUGTLT
greedy

TREACHEROUS = 3. OREEHARCUTS
dangerous; hazardous

HALLUCINATION = 4. IHUAIONTLCLAN
a vision; figment of the imagination

BIZARRE = 5. RAEBRZI
strange; weird

VIOLATED = 6. IDLEVAOT
broke a law, rule, agreement, or promise

VULNERABLE = 7. ABEVULNLER
defenseless and exposed

QUIVERED = 8. DRIEUVQE
trembled; vibrated

REGRET = 9. GRETER
a feeling of sorrow or remorse

REDEMPTION =10. NTRDIEPEOM
forgiveness through making up for a wrongdoing

MAULED =11. EAUDLM
injured by a savage animal attack

MANIPULATED =12. TEPDILAMUAN
controlled

HAGGARD =13. DAGRHGA
tired-looking; an unhealthy appearance

INVISIBLE =14. VBIILEINS
not able to be seen or noticed

SAVORING =15. AOVGNSRI
slowly and thoroughly enjoying something

Touching Spirit Bear Juggle Letters 4

= 1. DNUEER
   to bear or put up with

= 2. EMSZMREIE
   to put into a trance; bewitch

= 3. LTISDFE
   withheld; suppressed; ended by force

= 4. EDDROUHS
   hidden or covered

= 5. RNAEEGSVC
   one who gathers things thrown away by others

= 6. APESDMS
   twitched or seized

= 7. FEDDIE
   challenged; boldly resisted or went against

= 8. GNARGMICI
   making a facial expression that indicates disapproval, pain, or difficulty

= 9. DMCEKO
   made fun of

=10. TUTRE
   total; complete

=11. OUOOMNSOTN
   boring; lacking in variety

=12. IAVLEERTNTA
   a choice or another option

=13. EOGGRD
   stuffed with food

=14. AGDRGHA
   tired-looking; an unhealthy appearance

=15. STOREERHACU
   dangerous; hazardous

Touching Spirit Bear Juggle Letters 4 Answer Key

| | | |
|---|---|---|
| ENDURE | = 1. | DNUEER |
| | | to bear or put up with |
| MESMERIZE | = 2. | EMSZMREIE |
| | | to put into a trance; bewitch |
| STIFLED | = 3. | LTISDFE |
| | | withheld; suppressed; ended by force |
| SHROUDED | = 4. | EDDROUHS |
| | | hidden or covered |
| SCAVENGER | = 5. | RNAEEGSVC |
| | | one who gathers things thrown away by others |
| SPASMED | = 6. | APESDMS |
| | | twitched or seized |
| DEFIED | = 7. | FEDDIE |
| | | challenged; boldly resisted or went against |
| GRIMACING | = 8. | GNARGMICI |
| | | making a facial expression that indicates disapproval, pain, or difficulty |
| MOCKED | = 9. | DMCEKO |
| | | made fun of |
| UTTER | =10. | TUTRE |
| | | total; complete |
| MONOTONOUS | =11. | OUOOMNSOTN |
| | | boring; lacking in variety |
| ALTERNATIVE | =12. | IAVLEERTNTA |
| | | a choice or another option |
| GORGED | =13. | EOGGRD |
| | | stuffed with food |
| HAGGARD | =14. | AGDRGHA |
| | | tired-looking; an unhealthy appearance |
| TREACHEROUS | =15. | STOREERHACU |
| | | dangerous; hazardous |

Copyrighted

| | |
|---|---|
| ACKNOWLEDGED | showed a sign of awareness or acceptance |
| ALTERNATIVE | a choice or another option |
| ANCESTORS | family members who have lived before one's own time |
| AWKWARD | inconvenient; difficult; uncomfortable; clumsy |
| BANISHMENT | removal from society; exile |
| BIZARRE | strange; weird |

| | |
|---|---|
| BRANDISHED | waved |
| CEASED | stopped |
| COAXING | gentle attempts to persuade or influence |
| COMPOSURE | calmness |
| CONJURING | bringing to mind; recalling |
| CONSCIOUS | known to oneself; aware |

| | |
|---|---|
| CONSEQUENCES | effects or results |
| DAWDLED | wasted time; moved very slowly |
| DEFIANTELY | willfully or disobediently |
| DEFIED | challenged; boldly resisted or went against |
| DELIBERATELY | slowly; carefully; thoughtfully |
| EMERGED | came out |

| | |
|---|---|
| ENDURE | to bear put up with |
| FEIGNED | pretended |
| FESTER | to become an irritating, infected, sore spot |
| FREQUENT | often |
| FRIGID | very cold; freezing |
| GLUTTONOUS | greedy |

| | |
|---|---|
| GORGED | stuffed with food |
| GRIMACING | making a facial expression that indicates disapproval, pain, or difficulty |
| GRUB | food |
| HAGGARD | tired-looking; an unhealthy appearance |
| HALLUCINATION | a vision; figment of the imagination |
| HYPNOTIC | fascinating; having a sleep-inducing effect |

| | |
|---|---|
| IMPATIENT | unable to wait; not accepting delay |
| INCESSANT | constant |
| INEVITABLE | can't be avoided; bound to happen |
| INFERNO | a very intense fire |
| INGENUITY | cleverness |
| INSIGNIFICANT | not imporant; meaningless |

| | |
|---|---|
| INSTINCT | natural inborn ability |
| INVISIBLE | not able to be seen or noticed |
| IRKED | irritated; annoyed; bothered |
| IRRITATION | annoyance |
| MANEUVERED | steered or managed with skill |
| MANIPULATED | controlled |

| | |
|---|---|
| MAULED | injured by a savage animal attack |
| MENACINGLY | in a threatening manner |
| MESMERIZE | to put into a trance; bewitch |
| MIGRATE | to move or travel from one place to another |
| MOCKED | made fun of |
| MONOTONOUS | boring; lacing in variety |

| | |
|---|---|
| OMEN | a sign or warning |
| ORBS | round objects |
| PERSISTENT | not giving up; continuing in spite of obstacles |
| POTENTIAL | the ability or capability |
| PURSUIT | the act of chasing or going after something |
| QUIVERED | trembled; vibrated |

| | |
|---|---|
| REDEMPTION | forgiveness through making up for a wrongdoing |
| REGRET | a feeling of sorrow or remorse |
| REHABILITATION | the act of returning to good condition or normalcy |
| RELINQUISH | to release or surrender |
| RELUCTANTLY | unwillingly; with hesitation |
| REVERENTLY | respectfully |

| SARCASM | the use of words to express bitterness or mockery; scorn |
|---|---|
| SAVORING | slowly and thoroughly enjoying something |
| SCAVENGER | one who gathers things thrown away by others |
| SHROUDED | hidden or covered |
| SOLITARY | alone; singular |
| SPASMED | twitched or seized |

| | |
|---|---|
| STARK | bleak; bare; very plain |
| STIFLED | withheld; suppressed; ended by force |
| STUPOROUS | dazed |
| SUBMISSION | the act of giving in to a stronger power |
| TAUNTED | teased; blamed or scolded in an insulting way |
| TENTATIVE | very careful; with hesitation; unsure |

| | |
|---|---|
| TRANCE | the state of being semi-aware; in a daze |
| TRAUMA | painful damage |
| TRAWLER | a type of fishing boat |
| TREACHEROUS | dangerous; hazardous |
| UTTER | total; complete |
| VENGEANCE | revenge; punishment |

| | |
|---|---|
| VIOLATED | broke a law, rule, agreement, or promise |
| VOWED | promised; **pledged** |
| VULNERABLE | defenseless and exposed |
| WARILY | cautiously |
| WEARILY | in a tired manner |
| WINCING | drawing back or tensing the body or face |

Touching Spirit Bear

| IRKED | SAVORING | REHABILITATION | GRUB | MOCKED |
|---|---|---|---|---|
| ANCESTORS | TENTATIVE | ENDURE | SUBMISSION | INSTINCT |
| COAXING | HYPNOTIC | FREE SPACE | EMERGED | FREQUENT |
| MENACINGLY | BIZARRE | WEARILY | RELINQUISH | POTENTIAL |
| ACKNOWLEDGED | MANIPULATED | VIOLATED | INSIGNIFICANT | BRANDISHED |

Touching Spirit Bear

| RELUCTANTLY | TRAUMA | CEASED | CONJURING | TRANCE |
|---|---|---|---|---|
| BANISHMENT | DELIBERATELY | ALTERNATIVE | HALLUCINATION | AWKWARD |
| QUIVERED | GRIMACING | FREE SPACE | GLUTTONOUS | DAWDLED |
| SOLITARY | SCAVENGER | SHROUDED | REGRET | SARCASM |
| COMPOSURE | UTTER | STARK | TREACHEROUS | TAUNTED |

## Touching Spirit Bear

| MANIPULATED | TRAWLER | TREACHEROUS | ORBS | GORGED |
|---|---|---|---|---|
| DEFIED | MESMERIZE | RELUCTANTLY | SAVORING | SCAVENGER |
| IMPATIENT | MONOTONOUS | FREE SPACE | STUPOROUS | CONSCIOUS |
| REVERENTLY | TRAUMA | ACKNOWLEDGED | VULNERABLE | INFERNO |
| FRIGID | WINCING | ENDURE | DEFIANTLY | COAXING |

## Touching Spirit Bear

| IRRITATION | INSTINCT | INSIGNIFICANT | ALTERNATIVE | OMEN |
|---|---|---|---|---|
| HYPNOTIC | FEIGNED | FESTER | SOLITARY | SHROUDED |
| HAGGARD | INVISIBLE | FREE SPACE | QUIVERED | INEVITABLE |
| FREQUENT | CONJURING | MENACINGLY | SUBMISSION | TENTATIVE |
| CEASED | WARILY | VIOLATED | ANCESTORS | BANISHMENT |

## Touching Spirit Bear

| DELIBERATELY | MESMERIZE | PERSISTENT | STARK | MANEUVERED |
|---|---|---|---|---|
| COAXING | ANCESTORS | SPASMED | VOWED | CONSCIOUS |
| SUBMISSION | BIZARRE | FREE SPACE | HAGGARD | FREQUENT |
| WINCING | BANISHMENT | FRIGID | VULNERABLE | DAWDLED |
| MANIPULATED | GRUB | OMEN | DEFIED | SOLITARY |

## Touching Spirit Bear

| MOCKED | DEFIANTLY | UTTER | TREACHEROUS | WARILY |
|---|---|---|---|---|
| VIOLATED | MENACINGLY | CEASED | CONJURING | VENGEANCE |
| BRANDISHED | INFERNO | FREE SPACE | SCAVENGER | GORGED |
| TENTATIVE | TRAUMA | REGRET | RELINQUISH | STIFLED |
| ALTERNATIVE | INSTINCT | MIGRATE | POTENTIAL | TAUNTED |

## Touching Spirit Bear

| AWKWARD | INSTINCT | STARK | BRANDISHED | INEVITABLE |
|---|---|---|---|---|
| ANCESTORS | FESTER | SHROUDED | MONOTONOUS | EMERGED |
| MENACINGLY | ALTERNATIVE | FREE SPACE | HALLUCINATION | ORBS |
| BIZARRE | FREQUENT | INSIGNIFICANT | REDEMPTION | WARILY |
| DEFIED | ACKNOWLEDGED | SPASMED | REVERENTLY | CEASED |

## Touching Spirit Bear

| GLUTTONOUS | TAUNTED | INFERNO | SUBMISSION | TENTATIVE |
|---|---|---|---|---|
| QUIVERED | OMEN | IMPATIENT | FEIGNED | DELIBERATELY |
| SAVORING | ENDURE | FREE SPACE | INVISIBLE | STUPOROUS |
| COAXING | GRUB | PERSISTENT | STIFLED | TRANCE |
| VIOLATED | DEFIANTLY | TRAWLER | FRIGID | MESMERIZE |

## Touching Spirit Bear

| EMERGED | HAGGARD | SOLITARY | ACKNOWLEDGED | IMPATIENT |
|---------|---------|----------|--------------|-----------|
| ORBS | TAUNTED | SHROUDED | DAWDLED | TREACHEROUS |
| HALLUCINATION | INCESSANT | FREE SPACE | INSIGNIFICANT | TENTATIVE |
| COAXING | MIGRATE | BANISHMENT | TRAWLER | TRANCE |
| GORGED | RELUCTANTLY | VIOLATED | INFERNO | FESTER |

## Touching Spirit Bear

| VOWED | INEVITABLE | ALTERNATIVE | REHABILITATION | CEASED |
|-------|-----------|-------------|----------------|--------|
| SARCASM | FREQUENT | SAVORING | MONOTONOUS | STARK |
| MENACINGLY | COMPOSURE | FREE SPACE | VULNERABLE | GLUTTONOUS |
| CONSCIOUS | FEIGNED | DEFIED | WEARILY | INGENUITY |
| SCAVENGER | HYPNOTIC | AWKWARD | ENDURE | GRIMACING |

## Touching Spirit Bear

| BIZARRE | IRKED | DEFIANTLY | WINCING | TRAWLER |
|---|---|---|---|---|
| REDEMPTION | BANISHMENT | VIOLATED | SAVORING | FEIGNED |
| EMERGED | ANCESTORS | FREE SPACE | COMPOSURE | REGRET |
| CEASED | HYPNOTIC | CONSCIOUS | PERSISTENT | TREACHEROUS |
| MIGRATE | FREQUENT | VENGEANCE | IRRITATION | STUPOROUS |

## Touching Spirit Bear

| REVERENTLY | IMPATIENT | DELIBERATELY | CONSEQUENCES | INFERNO |
|---|---|---|---|---|
| INVISIBLE | GRIMACING | PURSUIT | INCESSANT | STIFLED |
| MONOTONOUS | RELUCTANTLY | FREE SPACE | SHROUDED | INEVITABLE |
| VOWED | ENDURE | MANEUVERED | TENTATIVE | INSTINCT |
| FESTER | UTTER | GORGED | TRANCE | OMEN |

## Touching Spirit Bear

| SUBMISSION | TRAUMA | TREACHEROUS | INCESSANT | BANISHMENT |
|---|---|---|---|---|
| TAUNTED | MOCKED | OMEN | INFERNO | RELUCTANTLY |
| MANEUVERED | STARK | FREE SPACE | CONJURING | MIGRATE |
| GRUB | QUIVERED | REDEMPTION | SHROUDED | TRANCE |
| DELIBERATELY | CONSEQUENCES | HYPNOTIC | RELINQUISH | MONOTONOUS |

## Touching Spirit Bear

| VOWED | FRIGID | DEFIED | GORGED | MENACINGLY |
|---|---|---|---|---|
| WINCING | DAWDLED | BRANDISHED | HAGGARD | ORBS |
| CEASED | ALTERNATIVE | FREE SPACE | SPASMED | FREQUENT |
| EMERGED | PURSUIT | SOLITARY | FESTER | UTTER |
| VIOLATED | IMPATIENT | ENDURE | VULNERABLE | REHABILITATION |

## Touching Spirit Bear

| | | | | |
|---|---|---|---|---|
| RELUCTANTLY | VULNERABLE | INCESSANT | MOCKED | FESTER |
| BANISHMENT | DELIBERATELY | FRIGID | ENDURE | TRAUMA |
| WINCING | SHROUDED | FREE SPACE | INFERNO | TRANCE |
| VENGEANCE | ANCESTORS | HAGGARD | DAWDLED | TENTATIVE |
| PURSUIT | REGRET | DEFIANTLY | TRAWLER | COMPOSURE |

## Touching Spirit Bear

| | | | | |
|---|---|---|---|---|
| STIFLED | TREACHEROUS | REVERENTLY | OMEN | CONSCIOUS |
| MANEUVERED | SOLITARY | SPASMED | UTTER | AWKWARD |
| PERSISTENT | CONSEQUENCES | FREE SPACE | VIOLATED | MAULED |
| DEFIED | TAUNTED | POTENTIAL | REHABILITATION | GRUB |
| COAXING | WARILY | EMERGED | ALTERNATIVE | ACKNOWLEDGED |

## Touching Spirit Bear

| MONOTONOUS | STIFLED | SHROUDED | HAGGARD | TRAWLER |
|---|---|---|---|---|
| HYPNOTIC | BIZARRE | DAWDLED | INSTINCT | INCESSANT |
| FESTER | ORBS | FREE SPACE | UTTER | WARILY |
| IRKED | MAULED | STUPOROUS | SPASMED | MOCKED |
| FREQUENT | FEIGNED | RELINQUISH | ANCESTORS | REDEMPTION |

## Touching Spirit Bear

| SOLITARY | MIGRATE | GRIMACING | TREACHEROUS | ACKNOWLEDGED |
|---|---|---|---|---|
| COAXING | CONSCIOUS | STARK | COMPOSURE | BANISHMENT |
| MESMERIZE | DEFIED | FREE SPACE | TAUNTED | WINCING |
| MANIPULATED | INEVITABLE | INGENUITY | VOWED | GLUTTONOUS |
| REHABILITATION | CONSEQUENCES | OMEN | WEARILY | IMPATIENT |

## Touching Spirit Bear

| | | | | |
|---|---|---|---|---|
| TREACHEROUS | MANIPULATED | VULNERABLE | RELINQUISH | PERSISTENT |
| GRUB | CEASED | SARCASM | DELIBERATELY | STARK |
| PURSUIT | DEFIED | FREE SPACE | TENTATIVE | TRAUMA |
| VOWED | SCAVENGER | BRANDISHED | STIFLED | HALLUCINATION |
| GLUTTONOUS | ALTERNATIVE | MIGRATE | WINCING | INSTINCT |

## Touching Spirit Bear

| | | | | |
|---|---|---|---|---|
| COMPOSURE | MENACINGLY | INVISIBLE | STUPOROUS | FREQUENT |
| DEFIANTLY | ACKNOWLEDGED | MANEUVERED | TRAWLER | MAULED |
| REVERENTLY | EMERGED | FREE SPACE | MESMERIZE | AWKWARD |
| WEARILY | MOCKED | REGRET | GRIMACING | FRIGID |
| IMPATIENT | COAXING | WARILY | QUIVERED | REDEMPTION |

Touching Spirit Bear

| DAWDLED | EMERGED | MAULED | VIOLATED | SPASMED |
|---|---|---|---|---|
| WEARILY | FESTER | WINCING | INEVITABLE | GRIMACING |
| STUPOROUS | ORBS | FREE SPACE | REDEMPTION | CONSCIOUS |
| DELIBERATELY | VULNERABLE | DEFIED | SUBMISSION | TRAWLER |
| SOLITARY | VOWED | STIFLED | SCAVENGER | INVISIBLE |

Touching Spirit Bear

| TENTATIVE | ALTERNATIVE | TRANCE | ANCESTORS | IRRITATION |
|---|---|---|---|---|
| FEIGNED | INGENUITY | SARCASM | FRIGID | GRUB |
| RELUCTANTLY | MANEUVERED | FREE SPACE | COMPOSURE | HAGGARD |
| BIZARRE | INSIGNIFICANT | PERSISTENT | TRAUMA | HALLUCINATION |
| STARK | INCESSANT | TREACHEROUS | SHROUDED | CONSEQUENCES |

## Touching Spirit Bear

| CEASED | REVERENTLY | DAWDLED | BIZARRE | REGRET |
|---|---|---|---|---|
| EMERGED | WARILY | QUIVERED | STIFLED | IRKED |
| INCESSANT | WEARILY | FREE SPACE | CONJURING | REDEMPTION |
| TRAWLER | BANISHMENT | GLUTTONOUS | STUPOROUS | MENACINGLY |
| STARK | PURSUIT | OMEN | TREACHEROUS | INEVITABLE |

## Touching Spirit Bear

| INVISIBLE | SPASMED | FRIGID | IMPATIENT | SOLITARY |
|---|---|---|---|---|
| UTTER | INSIGNIFICANT | MANEUVERED | CONSCIOUS | MONOTONOUS |
| RELINQUISH | VULNERABLE | FREE SPACE | REHABILITATION | FESTER |
| VIOLATED | INFERNO | SHROUDED | WINCING | DEFIANTLY |
| COAXING | MOCKED | BRANDISHED | ORBS | DEFIED |

## Touching Spirit Bear

| UTTER | OMEN | INVISIBLE | HALLUCINATION | TRANCE |
|---|---|---|---|---|
| ENDURE | DELIBERATELY | PERSISTENT | INSIGNIFICANT | STUPOROUS |
| HYPNOTIC | AWKWARD | FREE SPACE | REHABILITATION | WEARILY |
| VULNERABLE | SUBMISSION | STIFLED | MANIPULATED | TENTATIVE |
| SAVORING | TRAWLER | IRKED | FEIGNED | IRRITATION |

## Touching Spirit Bear

| MANEUVERED | ALTERNATIVE | REVERENTLY | ANCESTORS | COAXING |
|---|---|---|---|---|
| DAWDLED | INGENUITY | FREQUENT | MENACINGLY | GRUB |
| BIZARRE | REDEMPTION | FREE SPACE | TAUNTED | GLUTTONOUS |
| DEFIANTLY | PURSUIT | FRIGID | REGRET | MESMERIZE |
| INEVITABLE | GRIMACING | HAGGARD | RELUCTANTLY | DEFIED |

## Touching Spirit Bear

| | | | | |
|---|---|---|---|---|
| HALLUCINATION | ENDURE | REDEMPTION | DEFIANTLY | MANIPULATED |
| MESMERIZE | IRRITATION | RELINQUISH | WINCING | CONJURING |
| REHABILITATION | INFERNO | FREE SPACE | COAXING | WEARILY |
| PERSISTENT | TRANCE | SCAVENGER | PURSUIT | IRKED |
| BANISHMENT | FREQUENT | VIOLATED | VOWED | VENGEANCE |

## Touching Spirit Bear

| | | | | |
|---|---|---|---|---|
| STIFLED | OMEN | FESTER | MONOTONOUS | CEASED |
| INSIGNIFICANT | TRAWLER | TAUNTED | FEIGNED | CONSCIOUS |
| TREACHEROUS | AWKWARD | FREE SPACE | DEFIED | IMPATIENT |
| ORBS | SOLITARY | GRIMACING | SHROUDED | CONSEQUENCES |
| GRUB | POTENTIAL | BIZARRE | HYPNOTIC | FRIGID |

## Touching Spirit Bear

| DELIBERATELY | MANEUVERED | ALTERNATIVE | PERSISTENT | FEIGNED |
|---|---|---|---|---|
| AWKWARD | QUIVERED | TAUNTED | ANCESTORS | OMEN |
| EMERGED | BRANDISHED | FREE SPACE | CONJURING | TRAUMA |
| WEARILY | DAWDLED | HAGGARD | MONOTONOUS | INEVITABLE |
| MOCKED | GRUB | IMPATIENT | WARILY | INFERNO |

## Touching Spirit Bear

| BANISHMENT | VIOLATED | STIFLED | COAXING | INVISIBLE |
|---|---|---|---|---|
| GLUTTONOUS | REGRET | STUPOROUS | GRIMACING | ENDURE |
| INCESSANT | CONSEQUENCES | FREE SPACE | TENTATIVE | HYPNOTIC |
| TREACHEROUS | CEASED | VOWED | UTTER | WINCING |
| MAULED | BIZARRE | SARCASM | REHABILITATION | INSIGNIFICANT |

## Touching Spirit Bear

| | | | | |
|---|---|---|---|---|
| CONSEQUENCES | REGRET | TRAUMA | SHROUDED | PERSISTENT |
| SARCASM | WEARILY | ACKNOWLEDGED | MONOTONOUS | BANISHMENT |
| INCESSANT | BIZARRE | FREE SPACE | DEFIED | VIOLATED |
| ANCESTORS | MANIPULATED | WINCING | ORBS | REVERENTLY |
| GRIMACING | INSTINCT | FESTER | VOWED | CEASED |

## Touching Spirit Bear

| | | | | |
|---|---|---|---|---|
| STUPOROUS | SUBMISSION | VULNERABLE | AWKWARD | BRANDISHED |
| TRANCE | OMEN | COAXING | MENACINGLY | ALTERNATIVE |
| GORGED | TRAWLER | FREE SPACE | INVISIBLE | HALLUCINATION |
| COMPOSURE | CONJURING | WARILY | IRKED | PURSUIT |
| FRIGID | INSIGNIFICANT | FREQUENT | DELIBERATELY | MANEUVERED |

www.ingramcontent.com/pod-product-compliance
Lightning Source LLC
Chambersburg PA
CBHW081450070526
44586CB00019B/2294